SPOTLIGHT

P9-CEM-887

WISCONSIN'S DOOR COUNTY

THOMAS HUHTI

Contents

WISCONSIN'S DOOR COUNTY

DOOR COUNTY

Hold your left hand up for a moment, palm out. The thumb is, as the Depression-era WPA Wisconsin guidebook put it, "the spout, as it were, of the Wisconsin teakettle." That's the Door Peninsula. Early French inhabitants called the watery cul-de-sac formed by the peninsula La Baye (later, La Baye Verde, and finally, Green Bay). "Cape Cod of the Midwest" and other silly likenings (I've even heard "California of the North," and that *really* gets me going) are the rule here.

Incessant comparisons to Yankee seaside villages don't wholly miss the mark, though in spots the area smacks just as much of chilled, stony Norwegian fjords. Bays in all the colors of an artist's palette are surrounded by variegated shoreline—250 miles (more than any other U.S. county) alternately rocky beach, craggy bluff,

blossom-choked orchard, bucolic heath, and meadow. Door County's established parkland acreage—county, state, and municipal—is staggering, considering its size. Generation upon generation of shipbuilders, fishers, and farmers benefited from the magical microclimate here, and there's a predisposition within the populace not to get worked up about much.

HISTORY

Limestone bedrock here rises 220 feet out of Lake Michigan; it's part of the same Niagara Escarpment that stretches south to Lake Winnebago (and east all the way to Niagara Falls). Eons of waves have carved rough sea caves into the multihued red and smoky black cliffs. (The shores on the western side of Green Bay are dramatic in contrast—mostly

DOOR COUNTY

HIGHLIGHTS

LOOK FOR 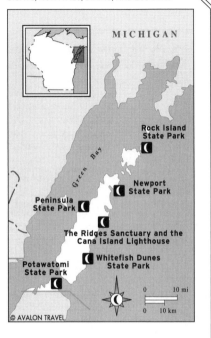 TO FIND RECOMMENDED SIGHTS, ACTIVITIES, DINING, AND LODGING.

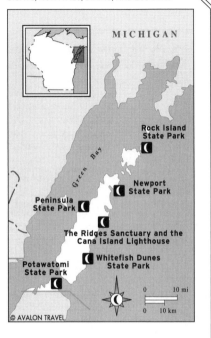 Potawatomi State Park: Overlook the historic waterways of the Door – all from a high perch atop the Niagara Escarpment (page 20).

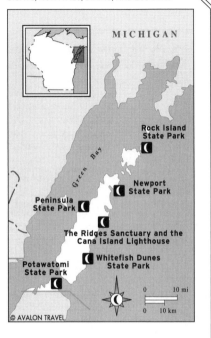 Whitefish Dunes State Park: On the wilder side, splendid dunes and critical habitat are here, formed by the rough wave action (page 21).

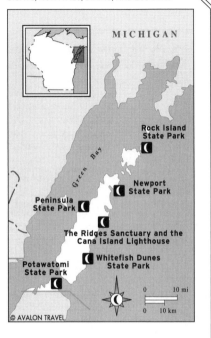 The Ridges Sanctuary and the Cana Island Lighthouse: A beloved sanctuary, it contains the grand, brilliantly white Cana Island Lighthouse (page 26).

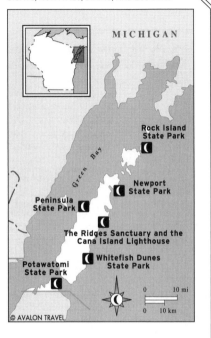 Newport State Park: Find preserved wilderness in one of the Midwest's most traveled vacation destinations. Yup, escape the madding crowds here (page 28).

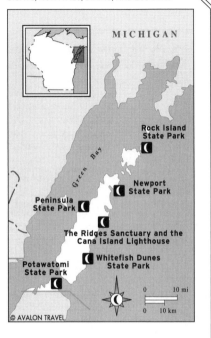 Peninsula State Park: This park is somnolent and picturesque, despite having tourist numbers rivaling Yellowstone's (page 35)!

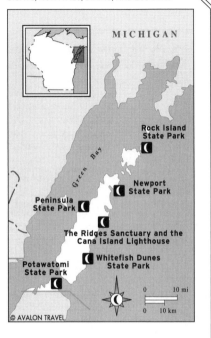 Rock Island State Park: This is as far as you get from anywhere in the state, an unparalleled "getaway" spot (page 50).

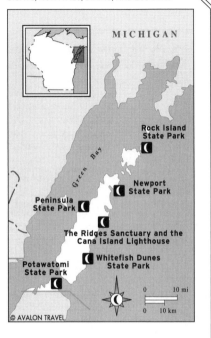

low-slung topography crawling toward the shore through marsh or beach.)

Porte des Mortes

At the tip of the peninsula is the only major gap in the escarpment, Porte des Mortes, the fabled "Door of Death"—so named by petrified early French explorers. The ferocious local climate has devoured hundreds of ships here. Accounts vary wildly (travelers will believe anything—and pass it along at the next inn) regarding which tragedy gave rise to the name Door of Death, but all are remarkably harrowing. Most accounts point to a band of 300–500 Potawatomi—some say Winnebago—who were dashed against rocks. Before the advent of modern navigation and large, diesel-driven screws, most ships could not overcome the shifting currents or conflicting wind shears (and shoals).

Human History

Human habitation at what today is Whitefish Dunes State Park dates back to 100 B.C. to judge by traces of the North Bay People, who spread from the mouth of the bay all the way to Rock Island. Woodland Indians arrived in the mid-1600s, when hostile, large-scale Iroquois expansion in Acadia forced the Hurons to flee. They likely arrived on Rock Island, which had been populated by Potawatomi, who would later return to open the doors to the Europeans. With the aid of Winnebago and Ottawa Indians, one of the largest ramparts in the New World was constructed on Rock Island to repel Iroquois invaders. (The U.S. government would later forcibly evict the Potawatomi from Rock Island so lumbermen could enter.)

On Washington Island in the late 17th century, the Potawatomi would initiate commercial

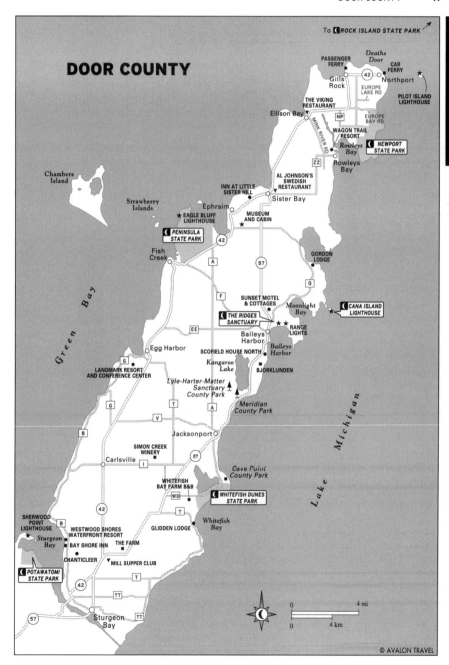

DOOR COUNTY

To ☾ROCK ISLAND STATE PARK

Deaths Door

PASSENGER FERRY
Gills Rock
42
CAR FERRY
Northport
EUROPE LAKE RD
PILOT ISLAND LIGHTHOUSE

THE VIKING RESTAURANT
Ellison Bay
NP
EUROPE BAY RD
WAGON TRAIL RESORT
Rowleys Bay
ZZ
Rowleys Bay
NEWPORT STATE PARK

Chambers Island

AL JOHNSON'S SWEDISH RESTAURANT
INN AT LITTLE SISTER HILL
Sister Bay

Strawberry Islands
Ephraim
EAGLE BLUFF LIGHTHOUSE
MUSEUM AND CABIN
☾PENINSULA STATE PARK
42

Fish Creek
A
57
GORDON LODGE
Q

SUNSET MOTEL & COTTAGES
Moonlight Bay
F
☾THE RIDGES SANCTUARY
CANA ISLAND LIGHTHOUSE
EE
Baileys Harbor
RANGE LIGHTS
SCOFIELD HOUSE NORTH
Baileys Harbor
Kangaroo Lake
BJORKLUNDEN
Egg Harbor
G
LANDMARK RESORT AND CONFERENCE CENTER
Lyle-Harter-Matter Sanctuary County Park
Meridian County Park
G
T
A
V
B
Jacksonport

SIMON CREEK WINERY
Carlsville
I
57
Cave Point County Park

WHITEFISH BAY FARM B&B
WD
☾WHITEFISH DUNES STATE PARK

Green Bay

Lake Michigan

SHERWOOD POINT LIGHTHOUSE
B
42
WESTWOOD SHORES WATERFRONT RESORT
GLIDDEN LODGE
Whitefish Bay
Sturgeon Bay
BAY SHORE INN
THE FARM
CHANTICLEER
MILL SUPPER CLUB
T
☾POTAWATOMI STATE PARK
42
T
TT

57
TT
Sturgeon Bay

0   4 mi
0   4 km

© AVALON TRAVEL

DOOR COUNTY DRIVING DISTANCES

TO THE DOOR
Chicago-Sturgeon Bay: 231 miles (4.5 hours)
Milwaukee-Sturgeon Bay: 145 miles (2.75 hours)
Madison-Sturgeon Bay: 184 miles (3.75 hours)

WITHIN THE DOOR (LAKESIDE)
Sturgeon Bay-Jacksonport: 15.4 miles
Jacksonport-Baileys Harbor: 7 miles

Baileys Harbor-Rowleys Bay: 15.5 miles
Rowleys Bay-Gills Rock: 7.5 miles

WITHIN THE DOOR (BAYSIDE)
Sturgeon Bay-Egg Harbor: 19 miles
Egg Harbor-Fish Creek: 6 miles
Fish Creek-Ephraim: 5 miles
Ephraim-Sister Bay: 4.3 miles
Sister Bay-Ellison Bay: 5.6 miles
Ellison Bay-Gills Rock: 3.9 miles

operations with Pierre Esprit Radisson, who considered the island one of his favorite sites in all New France.

Fishermen were the first to occupy most points along the Lake Michigan coast, including Rock and Washington Islands. Some of the largest fish ever caught on Lake Michigan were landed off Rock Island. Those communities, which also began commercial shipping and shipbuilding, cemented the regional economy in the 1830s. In shipbuilding, Sturgeon Bay always played second fiddle to Manitowoc farther south, but it still managed to parlay its ship factories into one of the major facilities on Lake Michigan.

PLANNING YOUR TIME

It's the quintessential weekend escape, yet let's make it a lazy, spiritual-battery-recharging week, which makes eminently more sense. If possible, try to schedule your arrival during the preternaturally lovely blossom season (generally beginning in very late April or very early May) or during an open-lighthouse period (generally concurrent with the blossoms)—wow!

Choose one place as a base of operations— **Sturgeon Bay,** for less driving time when leaving, or **Fish Creek,** for its centricity and because it's so darn cute. The county is also set up so that you go up one side and return along the other. (This author prefers to go up the more congested bay side and return along the more subdued lake side.) And please, don't forgo the somewhat forgotten county sibling— **Washington Island,** which itself leads to mustsee **Rock Island.**

Sturgeon Bay

The anadromous leviathans for which Door County's gateway community is named once crowded the harbor waters in such plenitude that ships would literally run aground atop heaps of them.

Whether or not Sturgeon Bay is properly the heart and soul of the county, it lies at a most strategic location: It was used for eons by Native Americans as a portage point. When the 6,600-foot-long canal was blasted, chiseled, hacked, and dug through to link the bay with Lake Michigan, the town of Sturgeon Bay was set. Besides the shipbuilding, most of the county's cherries are processed here.

More: The genuine graciousness of the folks is palpable. Sturgeon Bay was voted Wisconsin's Friendliest Small Town by those who really know—the readers of *Wisconsin Trails* magazine. Some jaded and wearied city dwellers are made uneasy by these folks, who

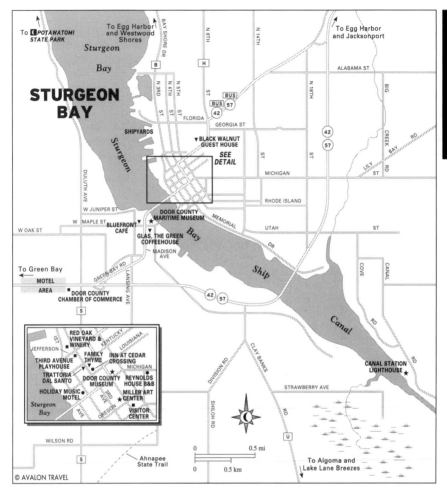

once pumped gas for this exhausted traveler while he rested in front of the station because he simply looked bushed.

SIGHTS

To while away some time pick up a map for a wondrous **National Register Walking Tour** of Sturgeon Bay, detailing more than 100 neighborhood edifices. Another personal fave freebie is to wander north of downtown to **Bay Shipbuilding**—a great place to espy behemoth

vessels as they're being launched or brought in for fixing. You can't get in the grounds but you can still get some good views.

Also check out great scenery along Lake Forest Road and Highways T and TT east of town. Wow!

Lighthouses

One of the oldest of its kind, dating from 1899, the **Canal Station Lighthouse** originally used an experimental design in which only latticework guy wires supported the tower and lantern. The station was redone after the turn of the 20th century, constructing the skeletal steel framework around the 100-foot-tall light. Access has become restricted now to the annual Lighthouse Walk weekend, but you can also see it from boat tours from Sturgeon Bay. If you arrive on wheels, the north breakwall is supposedly accessible, though views aren't all that great.

Ditto the restrictions on access for the **Sherwood Point Lighthouse** nearby.

Wineries

Given the county's proclivity for fruit production, perhaps it's not surprising that wineries have sprouted up every which way. Technically the only one *in* Sturgeon Bay itself is **Red Oak Vineyard & Winery** (325 N. Third Ave., 920/743-7729, www.redoakvineyard.com, hours vary), or at least the tasting room is downtown, where you can sample the wines from California grapes—and one local cherry wine. It's co-owned by a local Sturgeon Bayer who studied law before finally seeing the light and returning home to follow his passion, and good on him for it!

Eight miles north of Sturgeon Bay, in Carlsville, **Door Peninsula Winery** (5806 WI 42, 920/743-7431, www.dcwine.com, from 9 A.M. daily year-round, $3 tours) is housed in an old schoolhouse. Tours take in the cellars and winemaking rooms where 40 Door County California-style fruit wines are produced. A good eatery is attached.

An additional couple of miles along WI 42 to CR I (turn right) brings you to **Simon Creek Winery** (5896 Bochek Rd., 920/746-9307, www.simoncreekvineyard.com, 10 A.M.–6 P.M. Mon.–Sat. mid-May–late Oct., free tours), the county's largest and newest winery. There's an added bonus of live music Sunday afternoons. I love their Peninsula cream sherry!

Door County Maritime Museum

The Door County Maritime Museum (120 N. Madison Ave., 920/743-5958, www.dcmm.org, 9 A.M.–6 P.M. daily Memorial Day–Labor Day,

less often the rest of the year, $7.50 adults) is in a sparkling, 20,000-square-foot complex with splendid views of the bay. It synopsizes the shipbuilding industry, and kids love the periscope from a nuclear submarine; it's part of an ambitious exhibit on the crucial role Manitowoc played in building subs in World War II. Outside, you can also tour (10 A.M.–3:30 P.M. every half-hour during peak season, $5) the big ol' *John Purves,* a restored 1919 cherry-red tug.

Door County Museum

At 4th Avenue and Michigan Street you'll find a small museum (18 N. 4th Ave., 920/743-5809, 10 A.M.–4:30 P.M. May–Oct. daily, free) originally built by the WPA during the Great Depression. The *Chicago Tribune* called it the "Best Small Museum in the Midwest." The most popular attraction is the old-time firehouse, complete with refurbished pumper vehicles, including a horse-drawn model predating the end of the Civil War. Climb-aboard, hands-on vehicles are great for the urchins.

Miller Art Center

This fine art center (107 S. 4th Ave., 920/746-0707, www.millerartcenter.org, 10 A.M.–8 P.M. Mon., 10 A.M.–5 P.M. Tues.–Sat., free) is in the Sturgeon Bay library. The top floor houses the permanent collection, with an emphasis on 20th-century Wisconsin artists. One room houses Gerhard Miller's works.

The Farm

The Farm (N WI 57, 920/743-6666, www.thefarmindoorcounty.com, 9 A.M.–5 P.M. daily Memorial Day weekend–mid-Oct., $8 adults) bills itself as a living museum of rural America, and it lives up to that. On 40 acres of an original homestead, various old-style dwellings and structures dot the compound, and pioneer implements line the walls. The primary draw for families is the menagerie of farm animals—you can simply never tire of milking a goat, can you? You'll also find nature trails and informative displays about the diverse peninsular ecology.

DOOR COUNTY SPECIALTIES

BLOSSOMS

Flowers show up in mid-May and you're likely to be plowed under by camera-toting tourists here for blooming season. Cherry trees are lovely enough, but much of the county's cutover land and agricultural pasture has been left to regrow wild, and the county contains five state parks and the Ridges National Natural Landmark, a wildflower preserve with 13 species of endangered plants. The county is now also making a concerted effort to become one of the daffodil capitals of the world, planting more than 100,000 bulbs annually. Look for the white-and-peach-colored daffodil – I mean, doorfodil (seriously), developed locally.

Generally by the second or third week of May, blooms are peeking out. The bay side blooms first; the lake side follows a week to 10 days later. As soon as the blossoms are out, it's time for the **Festival of Blossoms,** a monthlong shindig of blossom field trips, midway rides, pageants, fish boils, shipyard tours (your only chance to see the operations up close), lighthouse tours, parades, and special cherry-centered celebrations.

LIGHTHOUSES

Door County has more lighthouses (people like to quiz you on this around here) than any other county in the United States. Starting in 1836 with Rock Island and in 1858 on Pilot Island (which can be toured only from the water), 10 lighthouses were constructed along the coasts and canals to hold Lake Michigan's stormy temperament somewhat in check. Almost all are still in some recognizable condition, and tours of some are offered regularly.

TOURS

A few resorts or lodges offer boat tours from their marinas; **Door County Fireboat Cruises** (120 N. Madison Ave., 920/495-6454, www.ridethefireboat.com, $20 adults) depart from the Maritime Museum and use a retired Chicago fireboat to chug along for two-hour cruises at 10:30 A.M. and 12:30 P.M. Memorial Day–Labor Day. The 10:30 tour travels through the Sturgeon Bay Ship Canal to Lake Michigan, while the 12:30 tour travels out into Sturgeon Bay to Sherwood Point and past its lighthouse. In July and August these trips definitely leave unless the wind is howling; in May, June, September, and October call ahead.

Harbor Lady (920/707-5239, www.harborlady.com) leaves from a resort and conference center complex opposite the Holiday Music Motel. For $15 to $20 you get a sightseeing cruise or a lunch (burgers and chicken) or dinner (buffet) cruise aboard a much plusher ride!

North of town, the **University of Wisconsin agricultural research station** is open for public perusal. Individuals can obtain a map for a self-guided tour of the 120-acre fruit and potato research center.

Too tired to hoof it? **Door County Trolley** (920/868-1100, www.doorcountytrolley.com) has an array of fun tours (historical, themed, culinary, and more, $14–65) on an old-fashioned streetcar. Check their website or phone for pickup points, which vary by tour.

ENTERTAINMENT

Sturgeon Bay is not a happening place when the sun goes down, to be sure, but there are options. The **Third Avenue Playhouse** (239 N. 3rd Ave., 920/743-1760, www.thirdavenueplayhouse.com) has a year-round slate of theatrical and musical performances in a renovated movie house.

One consistent place for catching live music is **GLAS, the Green Coffeehouse** (67 E. Maple St., 920/743-5575), with live music regularly but not on a set schedule. Oh, and in addition to good coffee and a lovely vista of Sturgeon Bay waters, it's got menu items as well. (The name, by the way, is Gaelic for "green"—yes, they get asked a lot.)

SHIPBUILDING

Given its welcome promontory jutting into the waters, 425 miles of shoreline, the safe haven of Green Bay, innumerable bights offering linked harbors, a plethora of native oak and, most important, a channel toward the outside world, it's no surprise that Door County became so important in shipbuilding.

As early as the 1830s, Manitowoc began to turn out oak sailing ships sturdy enough for the travails of the Great Lakes on the way to the St. Lawrence Seaway: the Wisconsin crowning achievement the Great Lakes schooner, a wooden ship with tight ends front and back that met below the water, a shallow draft, and a raisable centerboard, designed specifically to tackle Lake Michigan.

Door County to the north, meanwhile, had newer shipyards which didn't have to go through later refitting pangs – converting facilities to turn out steamships instead of clippers.

Sturgeon Bay churned out ships in amazing numbers. The first one left Sturgeon Bay shipyards in the mid-1850s, but it wasn't until the prime of the schooner days, in the mid-1860s, that the town really hit the big time. In the decade following the Civil War, perhaps two dozen famed ships were manufactured in the new shipyards.

The first major shipbuilder in Sturgeon Bay was Leathem and Smith, predominantly a ship-repair facility that opened in the 1880s. By World War I, it had expanded its operation into a prosperous boatworks and, during the Great War, produced more tugboats than any other outfit. Now called Bay Shipbuilding, it is still in operation in Sturgeon Bay. In fact, it's the number one operation, comprising a number of Sturgeon Bay builders in one grand merger, and can handle boats up to 1,100 feet long.

Many shipbuilders relocated here for the environment and abundant resources. In 1896, Riebolt and Wolter moved an entire drydock from Sheboygan. During the past half century, various corporate mergers have resulted in most of the Sturgeon Bay Michigan Street Bridge area's being an arm of one or more subsidiaries of the same company. Despite the decline in shipping brought about by the advent of railroad and autos, about 40 ships were still constructed during the decade and a half leading to 1986.

Peterson Builders, Inc., started just after the turn of the 20th century and constructed yachts, fishing tugs, and rowboats. Business boomed during the 1930s and the war years – 24-hour operations cranked out sub chasers and minesweepers. Today, the output includes wooden naval minesweepers, gunboats, torpedo retrievers, steel tugs, and landing craft.

The final jewel in Sturgeon Bay's shipping crown is Palmer-Johnson. Devoted to racing craft and custom yachts, it puts out million-dollar private vessels and acts as a repair facility. So renowned for yachts is Palmer-Johnson that offices and facilities have opened in four countries.

Up the road a piece, **Roadhouse** (5790 WI 42, 920/743-4966, Tues.–Sun.) in Carlsville, about eight miles north of Sturgeon Bay, has food, yeah, but it has often offered live blues performances Saturday nights July–October, though not last time we passed through town.

RECREATION
Rentals

Outdoor recreation equipment which doesn't require an engine can be rented from several outfitters. **Bay Shore Outfitters** (27 South Madison Ave., 920/818-0431, www.bayshoreoutfitter.com) downtown opposite—sort of—the Maritime Museum and other locations has rentals as well as guided tours. Figure $25 for a daily bike rental, more for a kayak.

Boats, canoes, and other outdoor gear can be rented from **Boat Door County** (920/743-3191), with several locations in Sturgeon Bay—the easiest being the Maritime Museum (120 N. Madison Ave.). Potawatomi State Park also has rentals, including kayaks.

Charter Fishing

Sturgeon Bay's sportfishing charter fleet ranks near the top five in the state in total salmon takes on a seasonal basis, but that's in numbers only. Factoring in relative populations, the Door Peninsula's communities are way ahead of the pack. Around here, lunkers prevail. The Wisconsin DNR says Sturgeon Bay charters have more fish per trip than any other north of Milwaukee, and a record 44.92-pound chinook salmon was landed (by a 16-year-old) off Sturgeon Bay near the legendary fishing spot called the Bank (as in bank reef); however, Algoma won't let you forget that it was from an Algoma charter boat. Most people don't know that the smallmouth bass and walleye fishing around here can be some of the best in Wisconsin, especially for flyfishing in late spring. As always, obtain a local list and do some advance work.

You can also contact the **24-hour fishing hotline** (920/743-7046).

Biking

Pick a direction and you'll find grand bike touring. This author loves to head up the lake side in the morning (starting from the Coast Guard Lighthouse—note that there can be lots of traffic on Highway T!) and then head back along the bay in the afternoon. The **Ahnapee State Trail,** best suited for mountain bikes but road bikes can handle it fine, starts just south of town and runs to Algoma. For non-deadly off-road riding, simply head to Potawatomi State park south of town.

ACCOMMODATIONS

Expect multiple-night minimums during peak season (and year-round if your stay includes a Saturday night). Unless specified otherwise, all listed accommodations are open year-round.

$50-100

A few of the cheapest motels may offer high-season rates in the $65–85 range for a single in summer; these dip much lower (as low as $45) in nonpeak times. However, most places cost much more than that.

Among the best budget choices—and yours truly's home away from home for more than a decade—is the (**Holiday Music Motel** (30 N. 1st Ave., 920/743-5571, www.holidaymusicmotel.com, $75). In 2007 a group of musicians—local and national, including Jackson Browne, I kid you not—came here to write songs for a benefit for the Michigan Street Bridge. Long story short, they loved the experience and the place was for sale, so what the heck, they bought it and rejuvenated it into a budget boutique kinda joint. You likely won't need the recording studio (don't worry—it's quiet), but your room has a fridge and new appointments. This is truly one of the best budget choices in Door County, odd history notwithstanding.

Then again, folks come here for cottage life, no? All the higher-end resorts have isolated cottages high on creature comforts. On the economical end, **Lake Lane Breezes** (5647 Lake Ln., 920/743-3463, www.lakelanecottages.com, $80 per day, $420 per week) sleeps 2–4 people. A very family-friendly operation, it's even got a tree house outside for the kids, and pets are welcome. It's southeast of town via Highway U (Clay Banks Road).

$100-150

At the (**Reynolds House B&B** (111 S. 7th Ave., 920/746-9771, www.reynoldshouse-bandb.com, $100–165), the ersatz anachronism of spinning parasols is eschewed here—it actually feels like a century ago in this antique-adorer's paradise. It emphasizes small but gorgeous rooms, superb service, and, was voted as having the best breakfast in the Midwest by no less than the knowledgeable readers of *Midwest Living* magazine.

A century-old commercial building (and erstwhile soda fountain), the **Inn at Cedar Crossing** (corner of 3rd Ave. and Louisiana St., 920/743-4200, www.innatcedarcrossing.com, $115–195) would best be described as Victorian country; the owner's flair and passion for folk art decoration is expressed in the rooms (room 6 is particularly warm and spacious). The inn also has a fabulous dining room.

You're not likely to find more welcoming proprietors than those at the splendid **Black Walnut Guest House** (454 N. 7th Ave., 877/255-9568, www.blackwalnut-gh. com, $145–160). The inn's four relaxing rooms are entirely different from one another—hmm, do you want the one with the spiral staircase to the hot tub in a tower, or the one with the double-sided fireplace?—but all are delightfully well-conceived. This guest house is very highly recommended.

North of Sturgeon Bay five miles via Highway 57, **Whitefish Bay Farm B&B** (3831 Clark Lake Rd./Highway WD, 920/743-1560, www.whitefishbayfarm.com, $125), a 1908 American farmhouse, has four sunny rooms. Instead of quotidian day jobs, the transplanted Milwaukeeans now raise Corriedale sheep. The farm covers 75 acres of meadow and orchard and with all that wool the owners, accomplished weavers, give spinning and weaving demonstrations in their barn-cum-art gallery.

Over $150

The restored farmhouse **Chanticleer** (4072 Hwy. HH N/Cherry Lane Rd., 920/746-0334, www.chanticleerguesthouse.com, $170–280) sits on a 30-acre orchard with gardens and sheep—yep, sheep. Find multilevel suites with 15-foot vaulted ceilings and private terraces, lofted suites with bisque pine ceilings and rafters, and a head-shaking array of amenities in each. Notable extras include a solarium, sauna, hiking trails, and a heated pool. I never met a person who didn't adore this place.

The **Bay Shore Inn** (4205 Bay Shore Dr., 920/743-4551, www.bayshoreinn.net, $199–310) has long been known as one of the most family-friendly resorts in the United States; it has three dozen luxurious kitchenette suites overlooking the bay, with a private beach. Just follow Highway B north out of town.

Not far away, quite a few folks have dropped a line to rave about **Westwood Shores Waterfront Resort** (4303 Bay Shore Dr., 800/440-4057, www.westwoodshores. net, $200-plus), with one- and two-bedroom suites with full kitchens, all of which have

commanding views of the bay. The suites have absolutely everything you could wish for, and staff friendliness is as noticeable as the views.

The 1930s **Glidden Lodge** (4676 Glidden Dr., 920/746-3900 or 888/281-1127, www. gliddenlodge.com, $235–390) was the epitome of hedonistic delight at the time—a massive, fieldstone main building offering stunning lake views. On the "quiet side of the peninsula," it's got a prime peninsular location. It's all suites, which all offer breathtaking lake views and magnificent sunrises. Follow WI 57 north to Highway T and turn right to Glidden Drive.

FOOD

The **Mill Supper Club** (4128 WI 42/57 N, 920/743-5044, dinner Tues.–Sun., $10–25) is a basic supper club with fish boils Tuesdays and Thursdays. Nothing flashy about it, but the food is great and the service has always been chipper as only found in a small town.

I'm most impressed with the newest restaurant in the Door: **Family Thyme** (136 N. 3rd Ave., 920/818-0520, 10:30 A.M.–8 P.M. Sun.–Thurs., 10:30 A.M.–9 P.M. Fri.–Sat., $8–15). A simple straight-up menu ranges from crafted (I think it's apt) burgers to southwestern-style kabobs and even a Thursday night world cuisine with, best of all, prices that won't break the bank. Better, it had taken over a bistro and the interiors will surprise you with some elegance considering the budget-worthy food!

West of the ship canal and a casually chic, energetic place, **Bluefront Café** (86 W. Maple St., 920/743-9218, lunch and dinner daily, brunch Sun., $8–18) defines eclectic. Where else in town to find pan-fried locally caught walleye next to a Thai vegetarian wrap? Yup, here. Try the fish tacos—it brings 'em in.

Phenomenal Northern Italian cuisine in a cozy but contemporary setting is right downtown at **Trattoria dal Santo** (147 N. 3rd Ave., 920/743-6100, 5–9 P.M. Mon.–Thurs., 4–9 P.M. Fri.–Sun., $12–25). This wonderful place has been honing its cuisine for nearly two decades and they've never overlooked anything in atmosphere. For this edition they added a new wine bar.

DOOR COUNTY FISH BOIL

Just when travelers think they've come to understand Wisconsin's predilection for fish fries, Door County throws them a curveball on the fish fetish – the fish boil, which is not at all the same thing.

Though Scandinavian immigrants came with their own recipes for fish soups and stews, the fish boil likely came from pure practicality. Door County had few cows or pigs, but it was rich with whitefish; potatoes and onions, hardy vegetables, were also abundant.

The modern version is a different story. As some tell it, the proprietor of Ellison Bay's Viking Restaurant concocted the first modern fish boil back in the 1960s, ostensibly searching for something unique to serve at the restaurant. It was an immediate hit that snowballed into the de rigueur culinary experience of Door County. Whatever the historical genesis of the boil, it has become a cultural linchpin for the peninsula community, almost a county ordinance.

THE WORKS

A Door County fish boil requires only a couple things: a huge witch-quality iron cauldron, firewood sufficient to blaze a light for Great Lakes ship traffic, and the innards – fish steaks, small potatoes, onions, and a heck of a lot of salt. Whitefish is for purists, but don't let that stop you from trying other varieties such as trout.

Add salt to the water and bring to a boil (the salt raises the boiling temperature of the water and helps keep the fish from flaking apart in the water). Add potatoes and boil for 15 minutes. Add onions and boil another 4–5 minutes. Add fish, which is often wrapped in cheesecloth to prevent it from falling apart, and boil for another 10 minutes. Now, here's the fun part: Right before the fish is done, use kerosene to jack up the flame to space shuttle-launch proportions. The kerosene induces a boil-over, which forces the oily top layers of water out of the cauldron to be burned off in the fire. Drain the rest and slather it with butter. The requisite side dishes are coleslaw, dark breads, and, this being Door County, cherry pie or cobbler for dessert.

An epicurean delight is the 🄲 **Inn at Cedar Crossing** (corner of 3rd Ave. and Louisiana St., 920/743-4200, 7:30 A.M.–9 P.M. Sun.–Thurs., 7:30 A.M.–9:30 P.M. Fri.–Sat., $8–32). Though quite modern and posh, the inn features original decor down to pressed-tin ceilings and ornate glasswork, and a fireplace roars in each dining room. The menu, heavy on fresh fish and seafood, emphasizes regional ingredients—as many foods as possible come from Wisconsin. Patrons swoon over the desserts with a somewhat alarming passion.

INFORMATION

The **Sturgeon Bay Visitor Center** (36 S. 3rd Ave., 800/301-6695, www.sturgeonbay.net) is downtown.

The **Door County Chamber of Commerce** (1015 Green Bay Rd., 920/743-4456 or 800/527-3529, www.doorcounty.com), just south of town, is generally full of all the information you're likely to need. It's got a 24-hour touch-screen information/reservation service. Otherwise, you'll find boatloads of local papers and other media.

One good website (www.doorcounty-wi.com) has links to other businesses and local media; another good website (www.door-countynavigator.com) is as much a sounding board for those who've tried local attractions, lodgings, and dining (that is, locals as well as travelers!).

GETTING THERE

Door County well represents the American antipathy toward public transportation. Hoi polloi disembarking from a Greyhound evidently doesn't fit well in a Cape Cod sunset postcard scene. There are no buses, no trains, and no ferries from points south. (Technically,

© THOMAS HUHTI

legendary views from Potawatomi State Park

one entrepreneur has floated a proposal to run a passenger-only ferry to Menominee in Michigan's Upper Peninsula from here, but this has been a rumor for years.) Sounds great? Wait till you see the traffic on a peak weekend.

Very small and very limited air shuttles from Chicago to Sturgeon Bay have occasionally popped up (none at present), but your real choice is to fly into Green Bay and rent a car or take the **Door County-Green Bay Shuttle** (920/746-0500, www.doorcountygreenbay-shuttle.com, reservations necessary), whose service does have a super-cool retro checker taxi!

◖ POTAWATOMI STATE PARK

Unfolding along the western edge of Sturgeon Bay and flanked by Sherwood and Cabot Points, Potawatomi State Park (920/746-2890) is known for rolling birch-lined trails atop the limestone ridges scraped off the Niagara Escarpment. The geology of the park is significant enough that Potawatomi marks the beginning of the Ice Age National Scenic Trail. You won't need a science background or superlative designations to appreciate its inspiring vistas and solitude; it is, simply, one of the peninsula's magical, not-to-be-missed natural retreats.

Almost 11 miles of trails wind through the park. An eight-mile **off-road bicycle trail** also meanders through grassy meadows. The great **Tower Trail** quickly ascends the ridges through thicker vegetation, leading to a 75-foot-tall **observation tower** and a belvedere vantage point of Michigan's Upper Peninsula on a good day (check out sunsets!). Islets rimmed in hues of blue and gray pepper the outlying reaches off the park (bring a polarizing camera lens on a sunny day). Fishing in the naturally protected bay is some of the best in the lower Door. The chilled waters also offer some fantastic scuba diving, with wrecks seen below.

Popular are the 14 miles of cross-country skiing trails and winter **camping** areas. Camping is popular as hell, so reserve the first day possible the winter before your trip; I'm not kidding. A camping cabin is available for disabled travelers. A park sticker is required in addition to the campsite fee.

For a quick road trip, head back toward WI 42/57 but turn right onto Highway C and then right onto Highway M, which takes you all the way to the **Sherwood Point Lighthouse** (it's a bit tough to spot). Built in 1883, this one took precisely one century to finally become automated! The 38-foot-high house guarding the bayside entrance into Sturgeon Bay was constructed with a 10-sided cast-iron light. Closed to the public, it and the old keeper's house are used today as a retreat for the Coast Guard. It is also open only during designated festival times, generally late May or early June.

Lakeside

Otherwise known as the "quiet side," this area shows less commercial development than the rest of the peninsula. The lakeshore side of the Door is a wonderland of pristine heath, healed cutover forest, rocky sea caves, some of Lake Michigan's finest beaches, biome preserves, picture-postcard lighthouses, and two of Wisconsin's best state parks.

The quick way into the area is WI 57, branching off WI 42 north of Sturgeon Bay. Farther off the beaten path, get right above the water along the coast starting southeast of Sturgeon Bay at the Sturgeon Bay canal North Pierhead Lighthouse. From there, an established State Rustic Road hugs the coastline all the way to Whitefish Dunes State Park, bypassing Portage and Whitefish Points and the Lilly Bay curve. Don't worry about getting lost once you find Highway T; there are no other roads!

◖ WHITEFISH DUNES STATE PARK

Some say Whitefish Dunes State Park (920/823-2400), approximately eight miles northeast of Sturgeon Bay, is the most pleasant park in the state system. The beach is indisputably so—miles and miles of

© DOOR COUNTY CHAMBER OF COMMERCE

Whitefish Dunes State Park

mocha-colored dunes sculpted into ridges by the prevailing winds.

The littoral site's proximity to inland lakes and creeks (nearby Clark Lake is more than 800 fish-rich acres) was likely the primary reason for settlement; eight temporary encampments or small villages date as far back as 100 B.C. European settlers arrived in 1840, when a commercial fishing operation on Whitefish Bay was begun by the Clark brothers (who lent their name to the nearby lake), working side by side with the Winnebago.

Today, everybody comes for the big dunes—among the highest on Lake Michigan, east or west. They were formed by numerous advances and retreats of ancient lakes and, later, Lake Michigan, and zillions of storms. Sand banks first closed off Clark Lake in what is now the mainland, and as vegetation took hold three millennia ago, wind deposits began piling up atop the sandbar. The result is a microcosm that couldn't possibly occur on the bay side of the peninsula—a wide beach rising to forested dunes. The tallest, Old Baldy, stands 93 feet high.

The one rule to follow dutifully is *stay off the dunes.* Many of the grasses holding together the mounds are peculiar to this park, and once they're gone, the dunes are done for (just take a look at the lifeless gashes created by motorcyclists before the park was established). Plank-and-rope boardwalks allow beach access on the **Red Trail;** at the midpoint, it branches away from the water to link with longer trails through mixed hardwood, red pine, or oddball wooded dune areas—13 miles in total. Continuing on the Red Trail to its southern end, hikers can reach the only climbable dune—Old Baldy, which offers panoramas of Lake Michigan and Clark Lake inland. From there, it's possible to link with longer trails. Farthest to the north, a short access trail to the White Trail leads to **Cave Point County Park,** likely the most photographed parkland in Door County.

From south to north in Whitefish Bay, the geology shifts from dunes to mixed sand and stone and, finally, at Cave Point, to exposed limestone ledges thrusting up to 50 feet above the water of the Niagara Escarpment—the bedrock of the peninsula. Eons of crashing waves have hewn caves and cenotes that show up as blowholes of sorts as the surf pounds and crashes, echoing like rolling thunder. The whole effect is not unlike the crumbled parapets of a time-worn castle. Sea kayakers have a field day snooping around this small promontory. Straight-faced old-timers tell of a schooner that slammed into the rocks at Cave Point in 1881 (true). Laden with corn, the ship cracked like a nut and spilled its cargo (true), and within a few days, corn had mysteriously appeared in Green Bay on the other side of the peninsula (hmm).

A caveat: Do not take swimming lightly here. The concave bend of Whitefish Bay focuses all the current, forming tough riptides. Predicting where these form is never entirely possible and *lifeguards are never on duty.*

This park is day-use only; no camping. Great picnicking, though, is found right atop the limestone ledges overlooking the lake. Do check out the nature center for its exhibits on the geology and anthropology of the area.

JACKSONPORT

You can always tell those who have explored the bay side of the peninsula first and then backtracked through Sturgeon Bay to come back up this side. Generally, these are the ones who race right through Jacksonport as if they didn't know it was there and then turn around to try to find what they missed.

At one time, Jacksonport rivaled Fish Creek as epicenter of economic booms on the Door. Once the local lumber was depleted, Jacksonport's docks were relegated to fishing boats. The last community to be settled in the county, Jacksonport caught one of the Germanic immigrant waves, and its annual **Maifest** (www.jacksonport.org/maifest) is among the larger shindigs held throughout the summer.

Somnolent Jacksonport today sports a few

© THOMAS HUHTI

shoreline view near Jacksonport

antique shops and gift cottages selling wares and crafts from dozens of Door County artists. A lazy strand of sand acts as a beach, and top-notch fun comes in the form of the sweets at the **Town Hall Bakery** (6225 WI 57, 920/823-2116).

Right downtown is the pinnacle of Jacksonport's developmental ambition: the **Square Rigger Lodge and Cottages** (6332 WI 57, 920/823-2404, www.squarerigger-lodge.com, from $80/100 s/d). More than a dozen basic but comfortable modern motel/condo units overlook the water (some do not), and most have private balconies or patios. One-to three-bedroom cottages also line the waterfront. They have lively fish boils here nightly in July and August, and four times a week in the off-season.

The supper club of choice is **Mr. G's** (5890 WI 57, 920/823-2899, lunch and dinner daily, $6–14), with a ballroom that has in the past had live entertainment, though most entertainment today comes from tall tales at the joint's Tiki Bar, part of the local bars' Yacht Club,

which is more Jimmy Buffett than America's Cup to be sure.

If that's too sedate, you may also have time for a margarita and some homemade salsa at **J.J.'s** (6301 WI 57, 920/823-2700) nearby!

BAILEYS HARBOR

Lake Michigan sportfishing really shows itself as you enter Baileys Harbor, every inch of road chockablock with trucks and boat trailers and a glistening new marina. It's a fitting legacy, actually. In 1844, a Captain Bailey and crew were foundering in a sudden squall when they espied this cove and took shelter. They were amazed to find a deep, well-isolated harbor and gorgeous cedar stands backing off the beach. So enthralled was the captain that he and the shipping company owner persuaded the U.S. government to construct a lighthouse at the entrance some years later. Thus, the first settlement in Door County was established. Its harbor remains the only designated Harbor of Refuge on the peninsula's lake side.

CALMER NEAR THE LAKE

Jacksonport, Door County, is on the 45th parallel, exactly halfway between the equator and the north pole, but don't let that fool you — the peninsula's climate is far more temperate than in other northerly Wisconsin areas. The ferocious waters of Lake Michigan, legendary for their unpredictability and furor, can also ameliorate the weather, keeping things cool in the dog days and taking the bite out of winter's Alberta Clippers. (Early weather accounts from Door County point out that the northern tip is generally a few degrees warmer than the southern end, though the bayside vs. lakeside difference is more important climatically.) This in part explains the rather one-sided habitation of the Door; most of the residents live on the western, or bay, side. With Lake Michigan in a huff, blowing fog, spray, and mist, Green Bay, in the lee of 15 miles of limestone windblock, remains sedate (if a bit cloudy). (Another oddity exists. Anyone visiting the vicinity of one of the Great Lakes will soon learn of "lake effect" snow, which is exactly as it seems. The waters can dump much more snow on the littoral edges than even a few miles inland, especially for those on the eastern shores. Looking at a map of Door County, surrounded by all that water, and you'd think it'd snow like a sonofagun here. Nope, Green Bay is not actually large enough to produce the necessary conditions, and as a result, Door County receives some of the lowest amounts of precipitation in the state!)

Sights

Before you come barreling into town, know that the sights around here are mostly south of town coming from Cave Point County Park. South of town along WI 57 at the southern end of Kangaroo Lake are my absolute undiscovered gems—**Lyle-Harter-Matter Sanctuary and Meridian County Parks,** which sandwich the highway and feature rough undeveloped trails past Niagara Escarpment rocks and one of the largest dunes in the county. (And remember as you sit and munch your granola bar, you're halfway to the North Pole!)

A bit south of town and along a splendid stretch of beach is a decidedly different kind of vacation, an educational seminar (from $1,000 with superb food, far less if living off-site) at **Bjorklunden** (7590 Boynton Ln., 920/839-2216), more a relaxed, soul-searching means of personal growth than a for-credit school experience (though it is the northern campus of Lawrence University in Appleton). Participants can live in a recently reconstructed Norwegian-style lodge built of local fieldstone and undertake courses in humanities and natural sciences. Some midweek seminars are also cheaper. Just to stay at the lodge, which looks like a Viking ship, is around $400 a week, meals included.

Visitors can tour from 1–4 P.M. Monday and Wednesday ($4) and check out the Norwegian *stavkirke* (church).

During the summer, the gardens of the estate host **Door Shakespeare** (920/839-1500, www.doorshakespeare.com), with evening performances daily except Wednesday.

In town itself, this author loves a simple pooch-led stroll along one of the county's longest sand beaches at **Baileys Harbor Park.**

The Town Hall (can't miss it) has the local **visitors information center** (corner of WI 57 and CR F, 920/839-2366, www.baileysharbor.com), open daily in summer and fall.

Recreation

Chinook salmon and rainbow and brown trout are the quarry for local charter boats, and the fishing in Baileys Harbor is some of the best in the county—Lilliputian Baileys Harbor (pop. 780) boasts a salmon harvest one-half the size of Milwaukee's.

Accommodations

Baileys Harbor has a couple of basic, modestly priced motels. I stumbled into the **Sunset Motel & Cottages** (8404 WI 57, 866/406-1383, www.baileysunsetmotelandcottages.

© DOOR COUNTY CHAMBER OF COMMERCE

Baileys Harbor

com, $75 and up) once and was most impressed by what you get for what you pay—as confirmed by a couple of other guests staying there. It's casual, rustic, but comfortable, with friendly proprietors—the way things used to be everywhere in these parts. It's just north of the Highway Q turnoff.

On the south side of town, there are above-average motel rooms and a lovely littoral setting to boot at the **Beachfront Inn** (8040 WI 57, 920/839-2345, www.beachfrontinn.net, from $90). In addition to a private beach, indoor heated pool, and regular campfires, this place gets many, many kudos for being so pet-friendly (they even have their own rescue dogs).

What may be the most enviably sited lodging in all of Door County is **Gordon Lodge** (1420 Pine Dr., 920/839-2331, www.gordonlodge.com, $160–425). Spread across the tip of a promontory jutting into Kangaroo Lake's north bay, the long-established Gordon Lodge sprouted in the 1920s as an offshoot of a popular Sturgeon Bay doctor's summer home. The main lodge has a lake view, while villas with fireplaces creep out right atop the water. Some original cottages are set back and nestled under the pines, which also drape over fitness trails. The dining room is casually elegant, and the Top Deck lounge, originally a boathouse, is unsurpassed for after-dinner dancing. Go north out of town and follow Highway Q toward the lake to Pine Drive.

The 1860s-era log home **Scofield House North** (920/839-1503 or 877/376-4667, www.scofieldnorth.com, $135–285) was painstakingly dismantled near Pulaski, Wisconsin, and relocated to the village, where it has become a showpoint lodging option. The gorgeous two-story log home has two bedrooms with skylights, two fireplaces, cathedral ceilings, and a lovely sunroom.

Food

The town has gone from basic fare to two road-trip-worthy eateries. Newest is **Harbor Fish Market and Grille** (8080 WI 57, 920/839-9999, breakfast, lunch, and dinner daily, $6 and up), a casually fine place in a 120-year-old building offering wondrous atmosphere. All comers will be happy; you gotta try the Wednesday and Friday (Friday only off-season) lobster boil! There's great custard and espresso next door.

Restaurant Saveur (8041 WI 57, 920/839-2708, 11:30 A.M.–3 P.M. and 5:30–10 P.M. Tues.–Sun., $17–35), very close by, is fabulously creative in its entrées that, despite flitting about the globe, are firmly rooted in the co-owner's South America (Chile to be precise). If nothing else, the restaurant would get my business for eternity for promising, when they opened, to be "creative, ambitious, elegant," and all those other usual things, but also to be "completely unpretentious." Done and done, and so it's become possibly the best new restaurant in Door County for this edition.

That said, some of us are old-school. If so, or if you're a Packers fan (rhetorical?), head immediately to **Weisgerber's Cornerstone Pub** (WI 57, 920/839-2790, breakfast, lunch, and dinner daily May–Oct., shorter hours off-season), which has three squares of solid comfort food (pan-fried perch since 1926) and quite honestly the best service during the last trip to the Door!

THE RIDGES SANCTUARY AND THE CANA ISLAND LIGHTHOUSE

Baileys Harbor is sandwiched between the strategic safe harbor on Lake Michigan and Kangaroo Lake, the peninsula's largest inland lake. Travelers are so preoccupied with these two sights that it's easy to miss the two large promontories jutting off the peninsula just north of town, forming **Moonlight Bay.** These two capes may be the state's most awesome natural landmarks and definitely have the most inspiring lighthouses. North along Highway Q is a critical biotic reserve, **The Ridges Sanctuary** (Ridges Rd., 920/839-2802, www.ridgesanctuary.org, trails open daily, $4 adults), 1,000 acres of boreal bog, swamp, dune, and a complete assortment of

wildflowers in their natural habitat. The eponymous series of ancient spiney sand ridges mark the advance of ancient and modern Lake Michigan. All 23 native Wisconsin orchids are found within the sanctuary's confines, as are 13 endangered species of flora. The preserve was established in the 1930s by hardcore early ecologists (such as Jens Jensen) in one of the state's first environmental brouhahas, incited by a spat over plans for a trailer park. The U.S. Department of the Interior recognizes the site as one of the most ecologically precious in the region; it was the first National Natural Landmark in Wisconsin.

The famed **Baileys Harbor Range Lights** are a pair of small but powerful lighthouses: a shorter, wooden octagonal one across the road on the beach, the other 900 feet inland—raised in 1869 by the Coast Guard. Three easy trails, ranging from just under two miles to five miles, snake throughout the tamarack and hardwood stands—20 miles in all and well worth the effort. Also on the grounds you'll find a nature center. Many have found the educational programs some of the best in the state.

Continue on Ridges Road to additional sites deemed National Natural Landmarks by the Department of the Interior and dedicated by The Nature Conservancy. **Toft's Point** (or Old Lighthouse Point) is along a great old dirt road that winds through barren sands with innumerable pulloffs. A few trails are found throughout the 600-plus acres that take up the whole of the promontory and include almost three miles of rock beach shoreline. To the north of the Ridges, the **Mud Lake Wildlife Area** is more than 1,000 acres protecting the shallow lake and surrounding wetlands. A prime waterfowl sanctuary, Mud Lake and its environs may be even more primeval and wild than the Ridges. Canoeing is also very popular, as Reibolts Creek connects the lake with Moonlight Bay.

And the bays don't end yet. North of Moonlight Bay is isolated North Bay, site of a handful of cottages and resorts. On the southern promontory you'll find undoubtedly the one lighthouse on the peninsula that everyone

© DOOR COUNTY CHAMBER OF COMMERCE

Cana Island Lighthouse, one of Wisconsin's most famous lighthouses

simply must visit, the **Cana Island Lighthouse** (10 A.M.–5 P.M. May–Oct., $4, and another $4 to climb the tower), accessible via Highway Q to Cana Island Drive to a narrow spit of gravel that may be under water, depending on when you get there. (Please note that this is a residential area, so really go slowly—blind curves are everywhere—and never, ever park inappropriately.) Impressively tall and magnificently white, the lighthouse is framed naturally by white birch. One of the most crucial lighthouses in the county, it stands far off the coast on a wind-whipped landform. Built in 1870, it was obviously considered a hardship station during storm season. North Bay is also the site of **Marshall's Point,** an isolated stretch of wild land completely surrounded by private development oft touted as a possible state park for its remarkable microclimate.

ROWLEYS BAY

Out of Baileys Harbor, WI 57 swoops back toward Sister Bay to WI 42. The next lakeside community, Rowleys Bay, is mostly a massive

and well-established resort and nearby campground, **Rowleys Bay Resort** (1041 Hwy. ZZ, 920/854-2385 or 888/250-7666, www.rowleysbay.com, May–Oct., $119–319 lodge/cottages). First of all, everyone still calls it "Wagon Trail," which until this edition was what it was called (the campground nearby was part of the operation). Originally a bare-bones fishing encampment and later a rustic lodge, the city-state has transmogrified into what is certainly the most comprehensive operation on the upper Door Peninsula. From semi-rustic lodge rooms (though these, with new management, will likely be gone) to posh suites, somehow the place does it all and does it well. Two- and three-bedroom rustically upscale vacation villas are set on wooded or waterfront sites; some can house a dozen folks comfortably, and all have whirlpools and fireplaces.

The contiguous, more or less, **campground** (920/854-2818, www.wagontrailcampground.com, from $37 for tents), spread throughout 200 acres along the bay, is really quite fastidious and professionally run. (It also offers cabins and even yurts!) Reservations are recommended.

Several miles of trails wend through the resort's acreage; one leads to Sand Bay Beach Park on Rowleys Bay, another to the Mink River Estuary. On the bay, the resort's marina offers bicycles, canoes, kayaks, paddleboats, charter fishing boats, and scenic excursions.

The reason most folks show up at the resort, though, is ◖ **Grandma's Swedish Bakery,** a magnet for sweet tooths from around the country hungry for 10 kinds of homemade bread, cardamom coffee cake, cherry pie, Old World–style bread pudding, and scads of muffins, cookies, and pastries. The specialty is Swedish sweets—*limpa* and *skorpa* (thinly sliced pecan rolls sprinkled with cinnamon sugar and dried in the oven). The resort's restaurant features all-you-can-eat fish boils Saturdays in summer.

Mink River Estuary

Stretching southeast from Ellison Bay to the edge of Newport State Park, the Mink River Estuary acts, by grace of The Nature Conservancy, to protect the river system as it empties into the bay through marsh and estuary. Primarily a crucial ornithological migratory site, the waters also act as a conduit for spawning fish. The topography of the 1,500 acres is astonishingly diverse and untouched; two threatened plant species—the dune thistle and dwarf lake iris—are found within the boundaries, and more than 200 species of birds pass through.

◖ NEWPORT STATE PARK

Not much is wild in Door County anymore, but the state's only designated wilderness park is here (go figure); this rough, isolated backwoods park (920/854-2500) constitutes half of the tip of the county, stretching for almost 12 miles along the Lake Michigan coast through an established scientific reserve—I might say it's a perfectly realized park. A remarkable diversity of hardwood and conifers, isolated wetland, bog, and even a few hidden coves along the lakeshore make the hiking appealing. Once

your best spot for isolation in Door County – Newport State Park

an up-and-coming lumber village in the 1880s, the town decayed gradually as the stands of forests became depleted. (Ghostly outlines of foundations are still scattered about in the underbrush.)

From wasted white pine cutover, the inner confines of the park are now dense tracts of bog forest. The southern section of the park is an established scientific reserve on 140 acres of mixed hardwoods. The park's magnificent ecosystem draws one of the planet's highest concentrations of monarch butterflies, which make a mind-boggling trip from Mexico's Yucatán Peninsula to San Juan Capistrano and then all the way here. Unfortunately, biologists have noted a dramatic drop-off in monarch numbers, mostly due to pollution and logging.

Trails

The park maintains nearly 40 miles of trails, along which you'll find wilderness campsites. By far the most popular area of the park is the northern tier and the two trails along Europe Lake—one of the largest of the county's inland lakes—a pristine, sandy gem uncluttered by development. With sandy forests and rocky beaches with great views of Porte des Mortes and the surrounding islands, it's got it all. Gravel Island, viewable from Lynd Point, is a national ornithological refuge.

In the southern section of the park, the **Newport, Rowleys Bay,** and **Ridge Trails**

alternately pass through meadows, wooded areas, and along limestone headlands on the coast, mostly along old logging roads. Spider Island, viewable from the Newport Trail, is another wildlife refuge for nesting gulls.

Fifteen of the park's trail miles allow mountain bikes, and bike camping is possible, though the park warns of porcupine damage to bikes overnight! Note that the trails are for the most part hardpacked dirt, but are regularly pocked with bikers' land mines—potholes of quicksand, python-size tree roots hidden under leaves, and more than a few spots of gravel (and porcupines). Essentially, anywhere that hikers go a bike can get to, just not always on the same trail. The most conspicuous off-limits areas are the shoreline routes—it's too tempting for bikers to whip down onto the fragile sands.

Camping

Here's the reason outdoor aficionados pilgrimage here regularly—there's no vehicular access to campsites. Sites are strictly walk-in (a modestly strenuous hike to some, a serious pack to most, but it sure beats the traffic death of Potawatomi and Peninsula; the shortest hike in is one-half mile, the longest nearly four miles). Two sites on Europe Lake are waterside, so canoes can land and camp; the Lake Michigan side has plenty of lakeside sites. Winter camping is outstanding here. As always, reserve way early.

Bayside

A preface, or perhaps, a caveat: WI 42 and WI 57 have been slated for (or, really, are endlessly being debated about) widening and straightening for years. South of Sturgeon Bay the road has already turned into mad swells of multilane madness. Thereafter, the leviathan transportation bureaucracy began eyeing stretches north of town. Grimly efficient, WI 42 north of Sturgeon Bay is approaching interstate whooshing.

WI 42 has perhaps the most intriguing history

of any country road. Not your average farm-to-market remnant, it was hewn from a tundralike wilderness in 1857 by starving millers and fishers desperate when winter arrived earlier than expected and froze supply boats out of the harbor.

On the way to Egg Harbor out of Sturgeon Bay, a great on-the-water side trip is along Highway B. Eventually, it merges with Highway G around Horseshoe Bay and leads directly to Egg Harbor.

EGG HARBOR

There's something of a contrived (officially, "revitalized") feel to Egg Harbor, back on WI 42. A couple of structures smacking of the early days are now redone with fresh facades. But there's more than a little new development, including an ersatz-Victorian strip mall that could have been plunked down in any city suburb or fringe sprawl in America.

This isn't to denigrate the lovely village at all, built on a rise overlooking one of the most accessible and well-protected harbors along either coast. The harbor had long been in use by the Winnebago before military materiel and trade ships necessarily anchored here—the only safe spot between Fish Creek and Little Sturgeon Bay. In the 1850s, Jacob and Levi Thorp, two brothers of the founder of Fish Creek, collaborated to build a pier to allow transport of local cordwood. By the 1890s, a rivalry with Fish Creek was born.

Oh, and that name. It doesn't stem from any ovoid land configuration but from a legendary 1825 battle between vacationing rich folk. While rowing to shore in longboats, boredom apparently got the best of the well-to-do, who started winging picnic-packed eggs back and forth. When the shells settled, a name was born. And they do celebrate this with occasional staged—and eminently delightful—egg throws, whether individuals or locally sponsored. (Yes, they do call the place—get ready to groan—an "eggscape.")

Sights and Activities

As you wind off WI 42 and down the hillside, your first sight is probably the most picturesque **village park** in the county, this one with a small strand of smooth-stoned and sand beach. There are free concerts Thursdays and Sundays in summer—lovely! Farther south a couple of miles you'll find an even better view of Horseshoe Bay and another very sandy beach at **Frank E. Murphy County Park.**

Just east of town a quaint, aged dairy barn now houses the **Birch Creek Music Center** (Hwy. E, 920/868-3763, www.birchcreek.org). Acoustics are extraordinary, considering the moo-cows who once lived here. Evening concerts by budding students and national names in the big barn are regularly scheduled (generally mid-July–Labor Day) and are something of an institution in the area—the big band series is particularly popular. Percussion performances are the specialty.

Sight of sights and a landmark for denizens of the Door is the Gothic revival **Cupola House** (7836 WI 42, 920/868-3941), a massive building constructed in 1871 by Levi Thorp, as local cordwood made him among the wealthiest men in the county. During the summer, resident artists at the Birch Creek Center give performances at the house; the mansion houses an assortment of shops and boutiques.

Ultra-premium wines (through micro-vinification, their word, not mine) are at **Stone's Throw Winery** (3382 Hwy. E, 920/839-9660), in a cool old barn.

The local library has a small visitors information center (920/868-3717, www.eggharbor-doorcounty.org).

Accommodations

The cheapest accommodations to be found in Egg Harbor will run you $90 or more, including the **Lullabi Inn** (7928 Egg Harbor Rd./ WI 42, 920/868-3135, www.lullabi-inn.com, $89–199) on the north end of town, the cheapest available, but you can expect a welcoming atmosphere despite the low bucks. Stay in small but clean value doubles, or upgrade through an array of larger rooms and apartments.

One of the largest resort complexes in the entire county, in fact Door County's largest resort, **Landmark Resort and Conference Center** (7643 Hillside Rd., 920/868-3205 or 800/273-7877, www.thelandmarkresort.com, $125–400) has myriad condo options, but all proffer spectacular views. You'll need both hands to count the swimming pools, another two for the tennis courts. There's also an excellent restaurant. It's easy to find this one—you can't miss it.

You'll find award-winning rooms at **Ashbrooke Suites** (7942 Egg Harbor Rd., 920/868-3113, www.ashbrooke.net, $154–249), with one- and two-bedroom suites done up in a French country atmosphere. It's just up the road from the Lullabi Inn.

Nonresort options abound in town. Try **Woldt's Intown Farmette** (7960 Church St., 608/873-8884, www.richwoldt.com, $125 daily, $500 weekly). This two-story cottage is adjacent to a reconstructed Dutch colonial barn and windmill. Turn east on Highway E, then a quick north jaunt onto Church Street.

Or, coming into town on WI 42, turn east onto Highway T for one mile to **The Cottage Retreat** (4355 Hwy. T, 920/743-4420, www.cottageretreat.com, $100–485 daily, $450–2,300 weekly). It has a reconstructed main cottage, lovingly put together from collected fieldstone. In fact, this place was green before green was in—built into earthen berms with southern glassed exposure, two of the main retreats are as cozy as can be. The sun-soaked two-bedroom cottage can sleep six and offers a combined kitchen/dining room/living area and a boardwalk to a Finnish wood sauna.

Food

All of the following are right on the main drag.

The early meal (and lunch) of choice is at the longstanding **Village Cafe** (7918 WI 42, 920/868-3342, 8 A.M.–10 P.M. daily) at the north end of town, a from-scratch place where you might find a vegan burger chicken fried steak tarted up Door County style with cherries and pecans.

Shipwreck's (7791 Egg Harbor Rd., 920/868-2767) has good pub grub but is really known as the county's only microbrewery (watch 'em brew as you quaff and you must try the Cherry Wheat Ales). Al Capone supposedly loved to hang with the lumberjacks here and used the subterranean caverns to beat a retreat.

The restaurant for gourmands in town, however, is ◖ **Trio** (4655 Hwy. E, 920/868-2092, dinner daily till 9 P.M. Memorial Day weekend–late Oct., $11–18), an eclectic and ambitious Italian and country French eatery serving fantastic antipasti and entrées. No bones about

it, this place gets raves from visitors for its Italian and French dishes. It's subdued in a lovely setting, yet kids are welcome and the staff have always been much praised. It's very well-done, and has been for many years now.

The **Log Den** (6626 WI 42, 920/868-3888, lunch and dinner daily, brunch Sun., $8–25), just south of Egg Harbor on WI 42, is a 10,000-square-foot place that actually feels less immense than that. The name is no misnomer, with wood everywhere, much of it ornately—at times cheekily—carved into a menagerie of anthropomorphism (I love sitting by the large lolling black bear). The menu runs from great—and moderately priced—burgers and sandwiches to ahi tuna, bluepoint oysters, and prime rib. The families that run the place have been along these shores and in these woods for more than a century and really give you an introduction to the place. And it's one of the most fun places to watch a Packers game, as well!

Then again, **Casey's Smokehouse & BBQ** (7855 WI 42, 920/868-3038, from 11 A.M. daily) is just about the perfect place to gorge on brisket or ribs after a long day of paddling or pedaling.

FISH CREEK

This graceful community offers visitors the anticipated coffee-table pictorials. It may be the soul, as it were, of the county, and yet, it's also "just" another Door County village—with a population right at 200.

Arguably the most picturesque view in the county is along WI 42 as it winds into the village from a casual bluff. The official village history describes the town's situation succinctly—"with its back to a rock and its face to the sea." A treasured stretch of road with a few hairpin perils, a roller-coaster gut-lifter, and suddenly you're in a trim and tidy Victorian hamlet that could have come out of a Currier and Ives print. Fish Creek boasts the most thoroughly maintained pre-20th-century architecture on the entire peninsula, about 40 historic structures.

In 1844, trader Increase Claflin, the first non-native permanent settler in Door County,

Fish Creek marina

left Sturgeon Bay after a few less-than-propitious incidents with the Potawatomi and wound up here. About this time, an Eastern cooper afflicted with terminal wanderlust, Asa Thorp, made his way to Door County, searching for his fortune. With his two brothers, Thorp constructed a loading pier and began a cordwood cutting business to supply steamships plying the coast. Later, Fish Creek transformed itself into the hub of commercial fishing on the Door Peninsula. Tourism was fortuitously there to take up the slack when the steamship supply industry petered out. By the late 1890s, locals were already putting out Tourist Home signs. Within a decade, even the home of Asa Thorp had been transformed into the Thorp Hotel.

Sights and Activities

Most visitors to Fish Creek prefer to simply stroll about, getting a look-see at the original architecture in an old county. The harbor area also has remnants of the earliest cabins. Even the remains of an 1855 cabin built by the founding Thorp brothers stands on the grounds of the newfangled Founders Square mélange of shops and restaurants in the village center; they were rebuilt after a fire as closely as possible to the original designs. Another landmark structure is its famous "haunted house," the 1875 Greek revival **Noble House** (intersection of WI 42 and Main St., 920/868-2091, noon–5 P.M. Fri.–Sat. mid-May–mid-June, noon–5 P.M. Mon.–Sat. mid-June–Labor Day weekend, $3). The Gibraltar Historical Association (920/868-2091) has **historic walking tours.**

The country's oldest summer theater, the **Peninsula Players** (north of Fish Creek off WI 42 on Peninsula Players Rd. inside Peninsula State Park, 920/868-3287, www.peninsulaplayers.com) perform a spate of Broadway plays and musicals in a gorgeous garden setting with bayside trails late June–mid-October, a tradition in its seventh decade. Reservations are recommended. Even better: relatively recent renovations include heated floors!

Less than half as old, but with boatloads of attitude, the tongue-in-cheek **American Folklore Theatre** (920/839-2329, www.folkloretheatre.com) is an acclaimed theater-and-song troupe as likely to perform their own rollicking originals (as in "Cheeseheads: the Musical" or "Guys on Ice," a paean to ice fishing) or a ghost story series as they are the works of the Bard. Performances are held May–mid-October, also in Peninsula State Park, and now include an autumn Town Hall Series performed around the county. Mixed with the zaniness, as the name suggests, is an admirable amount of state and national heritage.

During August, professional musicians from across the country assemble in Fish Creek for the annual **Peninsula Music Festival** (920/854-4060, www.musicfestival.com), which offers Renaissance, Reformation, baroque, and chamber ensembles, along with an array of thematic material. Nationally known folk musicians and touring troupes make an appearance at **Door County Auditorium** (3926 WI 42, 920/868-2787, www.dcauditorium.com); theater and dance performances are also held regularly.

At the north end of town, the **Skyway Drive In** (3475 WI 42, 920/854-9938, www.doorcountydrivein.com) is a throwback movie experience—it's charming to catch a flick under the stars with a Green Bay breeze wafting.

Perhaps the most, er, accessible winery in Door County, and one that focuses on the county, **Orchard Country** (WI 42 S, 866/946-3263, www.orchardcountry.com, 9 A.M.–5:30 P.M. daily, till 6 P.M. Fri.–Sat.) is a fave. The winery has award-winning county fruit wines, pick-yer-own fruits, sleigh rides, and a bunch more.

Without chartering a boat or flying your own plane, the easiest way to take in (but not actually step onto) **Chambers Island** across the Strawberry Channel is via twice daily **sailboat rides** (920/256-9042, www.friendlycharters.com, $40 per person).

The **Fish Creek Information Center** (4097 WI 42, 920/868-2316 or 800/577-1880, www.fishcreekinfo.com) is fully equipped to deal with your travel snafus or last-minute needs; trust me—I've given it lots of practice.

Recreation

Boat and bike rentals are available in town at **Nor Door Sport and Cyclery** (4007 WI 42, 920/868-2275) near the entrance to Peninsula State Park, which is the place to get a hybrid bike, mountain bike, or a single-speed cruiser. Plenty of other equipment is also for rent. In winter, you can rent cross-country skis and even snowshoes and ice skates. At **Edge of Park Bikes and Mopeds** (Park Entrance Rd., 920/868-3344) your moped rental includes a state park sticker.

Accommodations

The cheapest rooms in prime season are likely at two places. **Julie's** (4020 WI 42, 920/868-2999, www.juliesmotel.com, $79–106), near the state park, has basic but good rooms (and a super-duper café) and gets a nod for being pet friendly; well, they're friendly in general but you know what I mean. Figure ten bucks more for the most inexpensive but nice rooms at **Applecreek Resort and Cottages**

DOOR COUNTY CHERRIES TAKE ON THE NATION

In early 2010 ABC's *Good Morning America* set out in search of the best breakfast in America. After interminable hoo-hah that that generally involves, it came down to four, Fish Creek's White Gull Inn (specifically, its tear-of-joy-inducing cherry-stuffed French toast) pitted against three other friendly-though-they-should-have-known-better-than-to-try eateries nationwide. Come on, are you serious? The White Gull, natch, came out on top. Score one for the Cheeseheads (or Cherryheads up here)! In celebration, the inn also serves it daily now. It comes with a night's stay; you can substitute but honestly, why on earth would you?

(WI 42 and Hwy. F, 920/868-3525, www.applecreekresort.com, $90 and up); they've got loads of other room choices.

I've always had a soft spot for the **Fish Creek Motel and Cottages** (920/868-3448, www.fishcreekmotel.com, $98–245) at the end of Cottage Row, a block and a half past the stop sign off WI 42, given it was the first place I ever stayed in the county way back when. This amazing motel was actually built in Ephraim and boated around the point in 1981. Free bikes are a nice touch here. They had just completely finished remodeling the motel section at the time of writing.

Travel media scour every inch of the peninsula annually, looking to scoop others on an undiscovered gem, though they generally rehash the same old thing: the stately grace and charm of the ◖ **White Gull Inn** (4255 Main St., 920/868-3517, www.whitegullinn.com, $155–295). A proud old guesthouse since 1897, it's truly the grande dame of Door County. Rooms—a couple with private porches—are anachronistic but still plush; a few cottages and rooms in a cliff house are also available.

The dining room serves a spectacular array of continental, creative regional, and seafood in a country inn atmosphere that's not at all stuffy. And then there's that legendary fish boil, so popular that people swear they've made the return trip just to experience the boisterous one here, where it's made extra special by the boilmasters, who often preside over impromptu singing.

You'll find the most history of all at the **Thorp House Inn and Cottages** (4135 Bluff Rd., 920/868-2444, www.thorphouseinn.com, $125–205 rooms, $125–185 cottages), on lands originally belonging to Freeman Thorp, nephew to Fish Creek's founding father. The inn is backed up along the bluff overlooking the harbor. When Thorp perished in a 1903 shipwreck, his widow was forced to convert their new Victorian into a guest home. You'll get anachronistic-feeling B&B-style rooms at the inn or a great beach house, or quaint but modernized (just enough) cottages.

A main rival to the White Gull Inn is the **Whistling Swan** (4192 Main St., 920/868-3442, www.whistlingswan.com, $135–205). This one has the best local history—it was originally constructed across Green Bay in Marinette and scudded across the winter ice in 1907 to its present site. Five period rooms and two suites are available; the arched windows, fireplace, and high ceilings of the lobby are a draw for casual browsers in the shops on the main level.

The most unusual place you'll likely find in Door County is the four-floored **Silo Guest House** (3089 Evergreen Rd., 920/868-2592, $110), near the state park. It's got two bedrooms and is fully furnished. The top floor is the living room, which offers a grand view of the surrounding areas. July–August it rents by the week only ($525).

Food

Yours truly groaned upon hearing in 2008 that ◖ **The Cookery** (WI 42, 920/868-3634, lunch and dinner daily, breakfast Sat.–Sun., $4–26), a sunny café with great, healthy takes on standards, had suffered a devastating fire.

Thank God all were well and they decided to fight on. The low-key place is now a tad more upscale, but snobby it ain't—it's simply a well-thought through and well-run place that's always trying to do the right thing, whether for the earth, the village, or the customers. Breakfast packs the place on Saturdays and Sundays, and healthy options abound; even vegetarians aren't forgotten.

An admission: yours truly is no fan of pizza (he loathes tomato sauce). Surprising as heck then that he can't get enough of the pizzas at ◖ **Wild Tomato** (4023 WI 42, 920/868-3095, 11 a.m.–10 p.m. Sun.–Thurs., 11 a.m.–midnight Fri.–Sat.). Seriously, I've even had persnickety outstater foodie types rave about these za's. Eat local, act local and all that—they just taste incredible!

After weeks of supper clubs, this author was overjoyed to find **Mr. Helsinki** (Main St. above the Fish Creek Market, 920/868-9898, 5–11 p.m. daily, $7–22)—and not just because yours truly is of Finnish stock! Rather, this international fusion bistro specializes in, well, everything from crepes to a dash of Latin and a lot of Asian tastes and it does it well, right down to homegrown kaffir limes and Mexican epazote spice. You can even get a luscious vegan squash curry. It's a bit funky and irreverent and a whole lot of something else.

The food at the historic **Summertime Restaurant** (1 N. Spruce St., 920/868-3738, 7:30 a.m.–10 p.m. daily in season, $4–30) runs from fish to steaks, with a bit of Italian thrown in. The specialty of the house is South African back ribs. Seating? Your choice of a large hall, a loft dining room, or an outside patio. Built in 1910 as one of the original village cafés, it's definitely still got that old-fashioned feel.

Moving into the site of a longstanding supper club, **Cooper's Corner** (4172 Main St., 920/868-2667, 7 a.m.–11 p.m. daily, $7–30) fills those big shoes well and definitely takes the cuisine up a big notch. As many local products as possible are used in the creative dishes; they also smoke their own fish. The interiors were finished off with a lovely waterfall and al fresco dining. It's owned by the proprietors of the Door Peninsula Winery in Carlsville. (All that fine dining verbiage aside, their scrumptious breakfasts are very reasonably priced!) Having only been open a while, it'll have a break-in period for service, but it's off to a great start.

The White Gull Inn gets much-deserved press around the state—and, recently, nation—for its dining, yet for dinner you may not be able to beat the **(C** Whistling Swan** (4192 Main St., 920/868-3442, www.whistlingswan.com, dinner daily, $18–36). Expect gorgeous environs, gorgeous food (which of course is impeccably done), and a top-notch staff. This is a genuine treat.

(PENINSULA STATE PARK

Consider: 3,800 variegated acres stretching from the northern fringe of Fish Creek, past Strawberry Channel, past Eagle Bluff, past Nicolet Bay, and finally to Eagle Harbor and Ephraim. All of it magnificent. Deeded to the state for a state park in 1909, Peninsula is the second-oldest park in the state system, and with no statistical manipulation the park is numero uno in usage in Wisconsin. (Heck, it even draws more folks per annum than Yellowstone National Park!)

The peninsula, rising 180 feet above the lake at Eagle Bluff, is a manifestation of the western edge of the Niagara Escarpment, here a steep and variegated series of headlands and reentrants. The ecosystem here is unparalleled. Near Weborg Point in the southwest, the Peninsula White Cedar Forest Natural Area is a 53-acre stand of spruce, cedar, balsam, and hemlock, and the boggy residual tract of an ancient lake. South of Eagle Tower is the larger, 80-acre Peninsula Beech Forest Natural Area. Not only is this a primitive example of northern mixed hardwood, but it is a relatively uncommon stand of American beech. Within both confines is a handful of threatened species, including the vivid dwarf lake iris. Other rarities include gaywings, Indian paintbrush, blue-eyed grass, and downy gentian. Not impressed? You will be if you ever witness a sunset here!

Peninsula State Park

WORKING UP A SWEAT, DOOR COUNTY STYLE

For generations the Door was for weekend art browsers, beach lollers, or leaf-or-cherry-peepers, yet today you're as likely to see Lycra-clad gonzo type-T travelers with bike/kayak/ski racks atop the Subarus or Moby Dick-chasing boats behind the Suburban. Yep, Door County is actually a sublime place to get into or onto the land (or water).

Hiking is available pretty much everywhere, from nature trails to relatively ambitious backcountry hikes in the northern swaths of the county. One dream of this author's is to simply walk up one side of the peninsula, then head back on the other side, camping at public parks along the way. It's very doable.

Fishing has always been key here, whether it's a grandpa tossing a line for a smallmouth bass (this being one of the best places in the United States for the species), or, more commonly, a tourist heading out on a charter for trout or salmon (Sturgeon Bay especially for the latter). A real treat is helping the locals net tasty smelt around late April. There are far too many options for a book of this size; the county's chamber of commerce website (www.doorcounty.com) has very good links to whatever you need.

Then, there's **biking.** Yers truly is a biker, on and off the pavement. Really nothing in life is better than tossing away the book and map and just heading up any road in the county – you can't get lost. Better: the roads are mostly level here. Traffic is rarely too problematic, even on the main highways here, so you've also got Peninsula and Potawatomi State Parks for gorgeous and challenging on-road biking. The best off-road cycling in Wisconsin may come at Newport State Park.

The hidden gem to be sure is **kayaking.** It took some time to catch on, but there are more and more guides and outfitters in the county to help you experience the gorgeous waters around these parts. The rule, generally, for me is to stick to the bay side 'cuz I'm chicken of taking a kayak on a Great Lake, though Washington Island has wondrous paddling.

History

As usual, the first European, Increase Claflin, was a squatter; he parked his cabin high above the Strawberry Islands in 1844. But Plano Indian encampments have been examined and dated to 7000–4000 B.C., and the Menominee, Fox, Winnebago, Iroquois, and Potawatomi Indians have all occupied littoral sites. The Native American presence—and for once, overtly harmonious relations—is symbolized by the **Memorial Pole.** This 40-foot totem pole commemorates Potawatomi chief Simon Khaquados, laid to rest here in 1930 before thousands of admirers. Unfortunately, the settlers didn't love him enough to preclude building a golf course around his grave; the pole today sits between the number 1 and number 9 fairways.

Sights and Activities

Obligatory is the **Eagle Bluff Lighthouse** (920/421-3636) built during the Civil War by U.S. lighthouse crewmen as the second of the peninsula's lighthouses, a square tower about 45 feet tall attached to the keeper's house. It stands atop the bluff and can be seen for 15 miles; the views from its top stretch even farther. The prized assignment for lighthouse keepers in the peninsula, it had a commanding view and the best salary, the princely sum (for 1880) of $50 per month. Public interest prompted local historical societies to peel off 80 layers of paint and set to work refurbishing it in the late 1950s. Tours ($5 adults) are given in early summer and autumn every half hour 10 A.M.–4:30 P.M. Monday–Friday, with shorter hours the rest of year.

Two 75-foot towers were erected at the park's inception and used as fire-spotting towers (one was later removed because of dry rot). **Eagle Tower** was placed where it is simply because so many people wanted to spot a pair of long-term nesting eagles—the two for whom

© DOOR COUNTY CHAMBER OF COMMERCE

Eagle Bluff Lighthouse, Peninsula State Park

the bluff, the harbor, and the peninsula itself were eventually named. Ambitious visitors can take Minnehaha or Sentinel Trails in lieu of driving.

Before hiking, most visitors head to the **White Cedar Nature Center** (Bluff Rd., 920/854-5976, 10 A.M.–2 P.M. daily Memorial Day–Labor Day, shorter hours rest of the year) to walk a nature trail and view a host of exhibits covering the park's natural history.

Golf

Deemed by the golf press one of the gems of Midwestern courses, this 18-holer is plunked right in the eastern swath of the park. (It was built by a group of Ephraim businessmen in the early 1900s as a nine-hole course with sand greens.) Tee-time reservations are obviously necessary—as early as you can make them. Call 920/854-5791 for information.

Other Recreation

More than 20 miles of hiking trails network through the park and along the shores of the bays. Fifteen miles of on- and off-road bike trails exist, and a state trail pass is required on certain marked routes. What may be the most heavily traversed recreational trail—**Sunset Trail**—roughly parallels Shore Road for five miles through marsh and hardwood and conifer stands. At dusk it is definitely not misnamed. An extra few miles take in the littoral perimeter of Nicolet Bay and lead back to Fish Creek via back roads.

The toughest trail, but also the most rewarding, the **Eagle Trail** covers two miles skirting the harbor and a couple of natural springs and affords challenging scrambles over 200-foot bluffs. The easiest hike is the three-quarter-mile **Minnehaha Trail,** linking Nicolet Bay Campground and Eagle Trail.

You won't forget a kayak or canoe trip to **Horseshoe Island,** which has its own mile-long trail. A bit rugged and definitely isolated, it's a fave getaway.

Peninsula State Park has its own bike and boat rentals (920/854-9220) at Nicolet Beach.

Camping

Originally, camping was generally allowed in any direction the ranger waved his hand and cost from free to $0.50 per week. Today, the DNR receives up to 5,000 applications for summer reservations *in January.* At last count there were, let's see, tons of campsites—469 to be exact, separated into four sectors, but it'll still be tough to show up without a reservation and get one. Only one sector is open year-round.

Incidentally, this is one of the state parks that tacks on an extra fee for camping 'cuz it's so damned used.

EPHRAIM

As the map tells it, five miles separate Fish Creek and Ephraim, but you'd hardly know it. On the way north, as you pass the north entrance of Peninsula State Park, a modest jumble of development appears, and then vanishes, and shortly the fringes of beautiful Ephraim appear.

By the way, that's EE-frum. Another of those endlessly long Door County villages along a vivid harbor, Ephraim isn't the oldest community in the county, nor are its structures the most historically distinguished. But aesthetically it may have them all beat, and in many other respects, the community is the most perfectly preserved slice of Door County. The quaintness isn't accidental—for a while the village dictated via social pressure that all structures were to be whitewashed in proper fashion. And it stuck. The town is set along gorgeous Eagle Harbor. An enclave of pious fortitude, it was settled by Norwegian Moravians and christened Ephraim, which means "doubly fruitful" in Hebrew.

Sights and Activities

The oldest church in the county, the **Moravian Church** (9970 Moravia St., 920/854-2804), built out of necessity when the village founder's living room no longer sufficed, is, appropriately enough, along Moravia Street. It was built in 1857 out of cedar from the Upper Peninsula (local logs were too rough for such a sacred

house); they offer free tours of this church on Thursdays at 1:30 P.M. Also on Moravia Street, the **Pioneer Schoolhouse Museum** (9998 Moravia St.) doubles as a repository of local history. Local art displays, with various media represented from juried shows and chosen by local arts associations, are worth a view. The final historic structure along the street is the **Thomas Goodletson Cabin,** an 1857 original (inside and out) and one of the peninsula's first cabins.

Down off the bluff are the **Anderson Barn and Store.** The ruddy barn was built in 1870. During the summer, it's open for browsing; the salient square silo is a rarity. Built in 1858 by Aslag Anderson, one of the original Scandinavian settlers, it sports old-time store items along with museumlike pieces. All structures save for the church operate as one museum (920/854-9688, 11 A.M.–4 P.M. Mon.–Sat. mid-June–Aug., Fri.–Sat. Sept.–Oct., $3, $5 including tour).

Summertime **walking tours** of all the historic structures depart at 10:30 A.M. Tuesday–Friday (usually, but call to verify) from the Anderson Barn.

Recreation and Events

South Shore Pier, in the heart of the village, has a large number of water-based recreation and tour opportunities. Hour-plus catamaran cruises (starting at $28), including a sunset cruise, depart seven times daily aboard the *Stiletto* (920/854-7245). Or rent your own pontoon boat, kayak, Waverunner, paddleboat, or fishing boat from the **South Shore Pier** (920/854-4324). Other operations offer kayak and windsurfing lessons and rentals; one even has parasail rides, which was only a matter of time.

The highlight of the entire year in Ephraim is the Scandinavian summer solstice celebration **Fyr Bal Festival.** Bonfires dot the shoreline and fish-boil cauldrons gurgle to commemorate the arrival of summer. A "Viking chieftain" is crowned and then blesses the ships and harbor. The accompanying art fairs are less Norse in nature.

Ephraim's information center (920/854-4989, www.ephraim.org or www.ephraim-door-county.com), is right along WI 42. A 24-hour kiosk is there in season for last-minute motel scroungers.

Accommodations

Understated and good for the wallet, **Trollhaugen** (WI 42, 920/854-2713, www.trollhaugenlodge.com, $79–169) just north of the "action" in the village is part motel, part lodge and log cabin. It's in a quiet wooded setting with updated lodge decor. Splurge for the log cabin, though the rooms are what you'd expect (not bad at all).

Not far away from here, there are those who have insisted to me that the **Eagle Harbor Inn** (9914 WI 42, 920/854-2121, www.eagleharbor.com, $98–269) is, for dollar spent, the best inn in Door County, if not the Midwest. Now that's saying a whole big mouthful but if they're wrong, it's not by much. The elegant nine-room inn (with two multiperson suites) is antique-strewn and offers a sumptuous country breakfast in the garden. The one- to three-bedroom cottages on nicely wooded grounds are also very appealing.

I quite like—no, love—🄲 **Lodgings at Pioneer Lane** (9998 Pioneer Ln., 920/854-7656 or 800/588-3565, www.lodgingsatpioneerlane.com, $169 and up), which has themed rooms. This often results in embarrassing tackiness, but these are impeccably executed with kitchenettes, fireplaces, private porches or balconies, and superb detailings. And the owners get rave reviews from pretty much everybody. (So be nice to 'em!) By far this is the best new entry for this edition. It's north of Wilson's ice cream parlor, then right onto Church Street.

Food

There are precious few restaurants here; the lodges and resorts take most of the food business.

I'm generally on the manic run and so really appreciate **Good Eggs** (9820 Brookside Ln., 920/854-6621, 7 A.M.–1 P.M. daily May–Oct., $5–9), set back off WI 42, where you can build your own omelet, wrap it up in a tortilla (try the cilantro), and dash. Or sit at their tables and relax with the water view.

A step-up in price is the casually creative **Chef's Hat** (Hwy. Q, 920/854-2034) off the main highway. Pear and pumpkin soup and a sandwich pretty much sums it up.

The **Old Post Office** (10040 WI 42, 920/854-4034, breakfast and dinner only, $5–10) in the Edgewater Resort is known mostly for one of the biggie fish boils in the county, but also for Belgian waffles.

Another touted lodging dining room is **The Second Story** (10018 Water St., 920/854-2371, 8 A.M.–8 P.M. daily May–Oct., $5–12) at the Ephraim Shores Motel, offering family-style soups, sandwiches, quiches, seafood, a salad bar, and wondrous Norwegian meatballs. Foodie friends have opined that the dessert tray is worth a visit!

It's nearly a Door County law that you stop at **Wilson's** (9990 Water St., 920/854-2041, from 11 A.M. daily May–Oct.) old-fashioned ice cream parlor, right in the heart of the village. Opened in 1906 and serving pretty much ever since, it's got ice cream cones as big as bullhorns, as well as burgers and homemade soups and salads. (Stick to the ice cream.) You'll feel as if you're in a Norman Rockwell painting hanging out on the white-framed porch.

SISTER BAY

Sister Bay can sure get congested on a typical summer Saturday—symbolic of its status as the largest community north of Sturgeon Bay (though the population is a mere 695). It's also the only spot north on the peninsula where a minor mall reveals itself. Named for twin islands offshore, the bay—not offering quite the windbreak of Eagle Harbor—never got much notice from southbound steamers until Scandinavian settlers discovered the dense forest land in the surrounding hills and erected cabins in 1857.

Activities

Sister Bay's quaint village park, with one of the prettiest stretches of beach around, hosts

Sister Bay's Fall Festival

the huge **Fall Festival** and is the linchpin of a fine community network of parks, which offer regular doses of free big band, jazz, country, and folk concerts—one definitely each summer Wednesday afternoon. Also on the south edge of town is the **Old Anderson House Museum** (intersection of WI 57 and Fieldcrest Rd., 920/854-7680, tours: weekends and holidays mid-May–mid-Oct., free), a restored house dating from 1895; this baby was built in Marinette, Wisconsin, and dragged across the ice to get it here.

Bayshore Outdoors (920/854-7598, www.kayakdoorcounty.com) has daily guided kayak tours, along with rentals of cross-country skis, snowshoes, and bikes.

Accommodations

Getting a room for around $60 isn't too hard in Sister Bay—a Door County rarity! One of the cheapest motels on the Door is the delightfully rustic **Century Farm Motel** (10068 WI 57, between Sister Bay and Ephraim, 920/854-4069, $60 and up). A real country farm, it's got four individual units with TVs and refrigerators. There are no frills here, but it's almost homey nonetheless.

Also good is the rustic, century-old **Liberty Park Lodge** (north on WI 42, 920/854-2025, www.libertyparklodge.com, $99–144). The main lodge has rooms dating back to the Door's tourism beginnings, now lovingly redone. Also available are Cape Cod–style woodland and shore cottages. Overall, a rich balance of old and new. And for the price, you cannot beat it.

A definite hop up, and perhaps a steal, **Little Sister Resort** (10620 Little Sister Hill Rd., 920/854-4013, www.littlesisterresort.com, $115–220) sits in a cedar forest setting south of Sister Bay off WI 42 near a gorgeous bay. These very comfortable surroundings also cater to families. You'll need to brew some coffee to go through the mind-boggling array of cabins and chalets, but this place is worth the money.

Forty-five large (up to 600-square-foot) and attractive rooms are available at the

Country House Resort (715 N. Highland Rd., 920/854-4551 or 800/424-0041, www.country-house.com, $120–337). All feature refrigerators and private waterside balconies, and some have whirlpools and other miscellaneous amenities. The grounds cover 16 heavily wooded acres with private nature trails and a 1,000-foot shoreline. It's *just* south of the main "drag" off WI 42, then toward the bay.

Food

For the "only in Wisconsin" file: The **Sister Bay Bowl and Supper Club** (504 Bay Shore Dr., 920/854-2841, daily April–Jan., Sat.–Sun. otherwise, $4 and up) right downtown does have bowling. But, believe it or not, it offers one of the better fish *fries* around—great if you're wearying of fish boils!

Or, right nearby, the best sandwiches in the county, this author says, come at the **D.C. Deli** (10663 WI 42, 920/854-4514, 9 A.M.–8 P.M. Mon.–Sat., 9 A.M.–3 P.M. Sun., $9), a smokehouse and restaurant that had a brisket so good that it once made my legs wobbly.

The **Mission Grille** (intersection of WI 42 and WI 57, 920/854-9070, breakfast, lunch and dinner daily, $5–25) at the junction of the two big highways is an early-20th-century church-turned-cozy restaurant. It features unpretentious but superb New American cuisine and atmosphere (and wine list). Vegetarians aren't ignored. The summertime dining on a trilevel patio and veranda is one of the most relaxing dining spots around.

The name **Sister Bay Cafe** (611 WI 42, 920/854-2429, breakfast and dinner with varying hours Apr.–Nov., $3–14) is misleading. It's got your basics, but better, the creative dinners shine, and then there's a whole slew of authentic Scandinavian fare, including a Norwegian farmer's stew; red fruit pudding with cream; and beef and pork patties styled after a Danish dish.

The most famous ethnic eatery in the county, if not the state, is **[(Al Johnson's Swedish Restaurant** (702 WI 42, 920/854-2626, 6 A.M.–9 P.M. daily, $5–18), where cars regularly screech to a halt when drivers see the legendary live goats munching the sod

roof. The menu offers Swedish and American food. Pound after pound of Swedish meatballs is served nightly, and other favorites are the Swedish beefsteak sautéed in onions and lingonberry pancakes for breakfast. It's often standing room only, and the restaurant doesn't take reservations. It's so lively it prob'ly ain't yer best bet for a romantic anniversary dinner. On a sad note, famous Al passed away in 2010, a great loss for the county.

You'll find impeccably well-thought-out and executed "regional international" cuisine, and certainly a meal worthy of splurging on, at the **[(Inn at Kristofer's** (734 N. WI 42, 920/854-9419, from 5 P.M. Wed.–Mon. May–Oct., $15 and up). Tiny in size but eminently dependable in its fare, the inn is a highlight of any true culinary experience in Door County. Just a recent heavenly example: Chicken Roulade with local cherries and Japanese herb bread crumbs with a lingonberry (local) reduction. This place will wow you. The inn also gives gourmet cooking lessons.

On the north end of town, the **Waterfront** (10947 N. WI 42, 920/854-5491, 5–9 P.M. Tues.–Sun., $24–37) is run by a couple with three decades in the Door's restaurant business and is well-known for its seafood.

Information

Sister Bay has a quaint tourist information center (416 Gateway Dr., 920/854-2812, www.sisterbay.org) in a refurbished log schoolhouse.

ELLISON BAY

Plunked along the decline of a steep hill and hollow tunneling toward a yawning bay, Ellison Bay's facade isn't initially as spectacular as Ephraim's, the architecture isn't as quaint as Fish Creek's, and it's a fifth of the size of Sister Bay. Nonetheless, there is something engaging about the place. It begins with what may be the best view from the highway in the whole county. Atop the 200-foot bluff on the south side of town, you can see clear to Gills Rock, farther up the peninsula. Founded in the early 1860s, the village originally served as a hub for lumber, courtesy of the operations in nearby

© DOOR COUNTY CHAMBER OF COMMERCE

Ellison Bay's Bluff County Park

Newport State Park. As recently as the 1930s, the town's commercial fishery led Wisconsin in tonnage—perhaps the reason a local restaurant is credited with the first fish boil.

Sights

The name is often misinterpreted as an approximation of the 130 lovely acres overlooking the northern fringe of Ellison Bay (north on WI 42, then left on Garrett Bay Rd.), but in fact, **The Clearing** (12171 Garrett Bay Rd., 920/854-4088, www.theclearing.org) refers to something a tad more metaphysical—closer to "clarity of thought." A contemplative retreat for the study of art, natural science, and the humanities—philosophy is ever-popular—the school was the result of a lifetime's effort by famed landscape architect Jens Jensen. Much like contemporary Frank Lloyd Wright, Jensen's maverick style and obdurate convictions grated against the entrenched elitism of landscape architecture in the early 20th century. His belief in the inseparability of land and humanity was considered foolish, if not outright heretical, in

those early days. A Danish immigrant, Jensen arrived in the United States in 1884 and became more and more enamored of the wild Midwestern landscape while simultaneously cultivating his radical notions of debt to the earth and the need to connect with it despite living in a rat race. While in Chicago creating the parks that made his name, he began buying land around Ellison Bay. By the 1930s, everything had jelled into a cohesive plan, and he spent the next 15 years establishing his retreat according to folk educational traditions in northern Europe.

The grounds contain a lodge, a library, a communal dining area, and cottages and dormitories for attendees. Summer classes are held May–October and last one week, though some day seminars are also offered. Meals are included. Lots of group work, outdoor exploration, campfires, and other traditional folk systems are the rule. Fees, including room and board (except Thursday supper, when attendees are encouraged to explore the town for a fish boil), are around $500 a week in the dormitory, $550 a week in a double room. Nonparticipants can visit on weekends 1–4 P.M. mid-May–mid-October.

Ellison Bay has the grand **Bluff County Park,** three miles southwest along WI 42 and then off toward the lake. Nearly 100 wild acres atop 200-foot bluffs overlook the lake. There is no camping, but some rough trails (none to the water) wind through the area. You'll find some wowser views!

Accommodations

The best places to stay are actually in the vicinity of Ellison Bay. Just north of "downtown" and very good for the price is the **Parkside Inn** (11946 WI 42, 920/854-9050, www.theparksideinn.com, $89–129). The main lodge has basic but very clean motel-style rooms; there's a more upmarket guest house with one or two bedrooms as well.

Food

The eatery of choice in town—it is in fact the heart of the village—has for a long spell been **The Viking Restaurant** (12029 WI 42, 920/854-2988, 6 A.M.–9 P.M. in summer, till 7 P.M. thereafter, $4–15). Credited with filling that first iron cauldron with whitefish, potatoes, and onions, and brewing up a culinary tradition, The Viking sadly was damaged severely by a fire in September 2010, quieting the roaring kettle fire for the first time in decades. At the time of writing, the staff (and many locals) were feverishly working on reconstruction and expected to have it reopened by spring 2011.

 T. Ashwell's (east of WI 42 on Mink River Rd., 920/854-4306, 5–10 P.M. Wed.–Mon. May–Mar., $20–34) is another Door County bistro worthy of an extra nickel or two. Creative comfort food, unique nouvelle cuisine, and yes, it features sustainably raised local food as much as possible, and much more, all in a cheerily casual environment. Take in a Thursday, or *tapas* night; otherwise, it'd be a lovely surprise if you got there on a Chef's Choice night and let him do it all for you.

Information and Services

The smallest visitors center on the peninsula might be the closet-size information kiosk in Ellison Bay (920/854-5448, May–Oct.), across from The Viking Restaurant.

GILLS ROCK AND NORTHPORT

Out of Ellison Bay, WI 42 cuts east and then changes its mind and bends 90 degrees north again into the tightly packed fishing village of Gills Rock (pop. maybe 75) and the first of the ends of the road. Parked high atop 150-foot Table Bluff overlooking Hedgehog Harbor across from Deathdoor Bluff, pleasant Gills Rock is as far as the tourist road goes on the Door—that is, until you hop islands. Sleepy and quaint and known as the tip or top of the thumb, Gills Rock has the feel of an old tourist camp from the 1930s. Up WI 42 a couple of miles is truly the end of the line, Northport. (Incidentally, the sine wave turns of the highway leading to the ferry offer some splendid autumnal scenery!)

© THOMAS HUHTI

Gills Rock harbor

Sights and Activities

Door County's "other" maritime museum (this is an offshoot of Sturgeon Bay's) is parked on a little dusty side road in Gills Rock—the **Door County Maritime Museum** (12724 W. Wisconsin Bay Rd., 920/854-1844, 10 A.M.–5 P.M. daily May–Oct., $4.50 adults). This one features gill nets and more gill nets—or rather, the commercial fishing industry. The highlight is an old fishing tug, and there is plenty of other old equipment. Admission includes a chatty guided tour.

Capt. Mariner (920/421-1578) is ubiquitous in Gills Rock for wetting a line. Chinook salmon and German brown trout are the specialties, and the rates of $80 per person aren't bad at all. You fish virtually the entire time and with this set-up, solo travelers and novices can take advantage of Great Lake sportfishing, a service difficult to find on other charters.

You'll find the best views of the bay and solitude at the largest park in the county, **Door Bluff Headlands,** almost 200 acres of wild trails and woodland. From WI 42, take Cottage Road to Garrett Bay Road.

Scuba divers come to Gills Rock for underwater archaeology. No joke—beneath the surface of local waters lie more than 200 wrecks, and the State Historical Society has ongoing "digs" on its Wisconsin Maritime Trails project. (If you can't suit up, the local visitors centers have maps of land-based information markers pointing out wreck sites from shore; link up at maritimetrails.org.) The **Shoreline Resort** (920/854-2606, www.theshorelineresort.com) has dive charters, though you must have your own gear and already be certified. The resort also offers daily narrated **scenic boat tours.**

Washington Island Ferries and Cruises

The most luxurious way to Washington Island is a narrated cruise aboard the *Island Clipper* (920/854-2972, www.islandclipper.com), a 65-foot cruiser specifically designed by a Sturgeon Bay boatbuilder for the Death's Door crossing. A basic crossing ($12 adults) is available, as is a ferry plus "Viking Train" island tour ($24).

There are up to 10 departures 10 A.M.–5 P.M. daily in peak summer season.

Northport exists solely to accommodate the second of the ferry lines to Washington Island. This pier was established as an escape from fierce prevailing winds on the Gills Rock side. Northport, in fact, has eclipsed Gills Rock as a departure point to Washington Island, as it is virtually always free of ice and saves precious crossing time. Those who wish to drive their cars over to Washington Island will have to come here for the **Washington Island Ferry** (920/847-2546 or 800/223-2094, www.wisferry.com), which takes autos and passengers. It also hooks up with the Cherry Train tour of the island if you take the 9:45 A.M. or earlier crossing from Northport, 11 A.M. from Gills Rock. The schedule for the ferry is staggering; check the wall map. In high season, July–late August, 21 round-trips depart to and from the island beginning at 7 A.M. from the island, 7:45 A.M. from Northport (no early trip on Sundays!). The farther you are from this zenith chronologically, the fewer trips depart. December–January, only four trips depart per day; February–March there are only one or two per day, and vehicle reservations are mandatory. Call anyway for verification in the off-season. A car costs $25 (passengers not included), each adult is $12, bicycles are $4, and motorcycles are $15—all prices are round-trip.

Accommodations

Prominent in Gills Rock, the **Shoreline Resort** (12747 WI 42, 920/854-2606, www.theshorelineresort.com, $119) offers waterfront rooms with patios and a popular rooftop sun deck; the views are grand! Charter fishing tours and assorted sightseeing cruises (the sunset cruise is perennially popular) also leave the on-site marina. It also rents bikes.

Unheard-of **On the Rocks Cliffside Lodge** (849 Wisconsin Bay Rd., 920/854-4907, www.cliffsidelodge.com, Apr.–Nov., $350 and up) is possibly the most private Door County experience; you simply have to eyeball it for yourself. This jewel is a massive 3,500-square-foot A-frame lodge with fieldstone fireplace atop a

60-foot cliff. It was overwhelming enough for *National Geographic* to feature it. Rates start at $350 a night for two people, but this sucker holds up to 18 (for $775)!

Food

The best food you're going to get in Gills Rock is some of that grand smoked Lake Michigan fish at **Charlie's Smokehouse** (12731 WI 42, 920/854-2972), whose proprietor or family have been doing it since 1932. The **Shoreline Resort** (12747 WI 42, 920/854-2606, www.theshorelineresort. com, lunch and dinner daily May–Oct.) is the other dining option, with good whitefish and basic hearty fare.

Washington Island and Rock Island

Rustic, time-locked Washington Island, an easy (and safe) ferry ride from the mainland across Death's Door, very nearly wasn't included as part of the Door, but in 1925, the Supreme Court ruled in Wisconsin's favor in a border dispute with Michigan. At issue were a number of the dozen or so islands in the Grand Traverse Chain, of which Washington and the surrounding islands are a part.

The island isn't what most expect. Many envision a candy-facade Mackinac Island, full of historically garbed docents or fudge sellers every two steps. Not at all. It's populated by 650 permanent residents, and development is absolutely unobtrusive. The place has a pleasant weatherbeaten seaside look to it, rather than the sheen of a slick resort. Best of all, Washington Island has the feel of a small Midwestern town, right down to the well-used community ballparks. This explains the island's perfectly apt PR tout line: "North of the Tension Line."

HISTORY
Natural History

Beyond Washington Island is one of the Niagara Escarpment's longest gaps as it stretches under the waters to Michigan and on to Ontario. Of the islands stretching across the lake to Michigan's Upper Peninsula, Washington is the granddaddy, geologically and historically. With 36 square miles, the island's circumference is just over 25 miles. The escarpment is on a consistent, gradual declivity (2–5 degrees), a mere 160 feet above the lake's surface, surrounding Washington Island's rough, wave-battered exterior. Nowhere on the Door Peninsula does nature manifest itself with more force—wind-whipped stretches of open meadow or scattered hardwoods equally wind-bent—than on this tough island.

Human History

The Door, a macabre caveat of death for those foolhardy enough to attempt the savage waters here, fits Washington Island, truly the door to Wisconsin. Washington and Rock Islands were populated long before the rest of northeastern Wisconsin. Before vandals and thickets of ambitious brush got ahold of the sites, the island was one of the richest Native American archaeological time capsules in the Midwest. The original island dwellers were likely the Potawatomi and later the Huron (the island's original name was Huron Island), among others, who arrived in flight from the bellicose Iroquois in modern Quebec.

Island-hopping voyageurs plying the expanses of New France found a ready-made chain of havens and temporary fishing grounds stretching from Michigan to the Door Peninsula, and thus to the Fox and Wisconsin Riverways. Purportedly, Jean Nicolet himself was the first European to set up camp on Washington Island. Pierre Esprit Radisson, who wintered here with the Huron, dubbed it the most pleasant place he had experienced in the Great Lakes. The most famous European presence still lends itself to the murky legends swirling in the cruel straits. In 1679, Robert

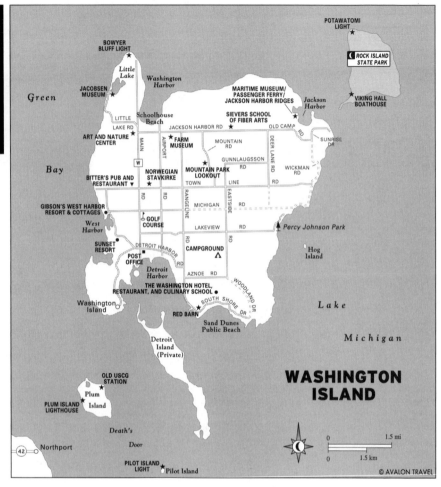

WASHINGTON ISLAND

La Salle sailed the *Griffin* into Detroit Harbor, where he met and bartered fur and iron wares with the Potawatomi and then left, destined for Mackinac Island. The ship vanished, and mariners have regaled the gullible with stories of a shrouded ship matching its description haunting the shoals around the Door ever since.

A large-scale European presence appeared in the early 1830s, when immigrants into Green Bay heard of trout the size of calves being taken from the waters around the island. The first fishers were Irish, but the true habitation mark on Washington Island is pure Icelandic—richest in the United States. Several thousand of the nation's first Icelandic settlers arrived, took readily to the isolation, and set down permanent roots. Their heritage is clearly manifest in the *stavkirke*—the wooded stave church—being built gradually by island residents, one massive white pine log at a time, and by the proud Icelandic horses roaming certain island pastures.

SIGHTS

There is a lighthouse on Washington Island, the **Bowyer Bluff light** on the northwest side. Unfortunately, you can't see it, but you may wish you could—at 210 feet, it's the tallest on the Great Lakes.

Art and Nature Center

A mix of natural and cultural island history is displayed here (1799 Main Rd., 920/847-2025, 10:30 A.M.–4:30 P.M. Mon.–Fri., 11:30 A.M.–4:30 P.M. Sun. mid-June–mid-Sept., shorter hours after Labor Day, $1 adults), at the corner of Main and Jackson Harbor Road in an unassuming building resembling an old schoolhouse. Permanent artwork displays are housed within, and nature trails branch from the rear. Art classes are offered, and regular musical events are held during a weeklong midsummer festival.

Museums

The top stop for museum hoppers is the **Maritime Museum** (10 A.M.–4 P.M. Mon.–Fri. Memorial Day–Oct., with some weeks open daily in summer, donations) at the east end of Jackson Harbor Road, opposite the ferry landing. The museum retains a significant presence—what little remains of the island's commercial fishing industry operates out of secluded Jackson Harbor. You'll find a reconstructed fish shed, a couple of ice houses, an old fisherman's house, some outdoor displays (a Kahlenberg engine, an old Coast Guard boat, and remnants of a wreck), and the site itself, housed inside two fishing shacks.

The **Jacobsen Museum** (920/847-2213, 10 A.M.–4 P.M. daily Memorial Day weekend–mid-Oct., donations) is housed in a vertical log building owned by early settler Jens Jacobsen, on the south shore of Little Lake. The packrat progenitor collected a huge number of natural history artifacts, mostly Native American arrowheads and beads. Also inside you'll find Danish scrollwork, maps, models of shipwrecks, fossils, and tools. There's also a whole bunch of weird stuff lying out front, such as an ancient leviathan rudder from the steamer *Louisiana,* which ran aground in 1913; ice cutters; and huge capstans for raising anchors.

The smallest of all is the **Farm Museum** (920/847-2577, hours vary, June–Oct., free), a spread of pioneer structures off Airport Road along Jackson Harbor Road. A pioneer log home, a double log barn and shed with a collection of hand tools, 15 pieces of horse-drawn machinery, a forge and blacksmith shop, a reconstructed stone building, and a popular petting zoo are on the grounds. Regularly scheduled kids' and families' farm activities starting on Wednesdays after July 5 and running through mid-August are a hoot.

Sievers School of Fiber Arts

In its second decade, the Sievers School of Fiber Arts (Jackson Harbor Rd., 920/847-2264, www.sieversschool.com) is the most intriguing of island highlights. It's less a school than a retreat into weaving, papermaking, spinning, basketweaving, batik, tapestry, drafting, Scandinavian woodcarving, and any other number of classes in vanishing folk arts. On any given day, the solitude is accentuated by the thwack of looms or the whirring of spinning wheels. Classes are offered May–October, and weekend or one-week classes are available. Fees range $190–340, plus up to $120 for dorm fees for a weeklong class. A downtown consignment shop displays and sells the works created as well as cherrywood looms.

Dunes

No visit to the Maritime Museum is complete without a stroll on the nature trail through the ecosystem of the **Jackson Harbor Ridges,** a 90-acre State of Wisconsin Scientific Reserve. The fragile mix of shore meadow, dune, and boreal forest is not found anywhere else in the peninsula. Northern plant species such as the rare dwarf lake orchid and arctic primrose, along with white cedar, fir, and spruce, are found here. A part of the ridges was established with a Nature Conservancy tract. There is an isolated and generally underpopulated beach adjacent to the reserve.

More great Lawrence of Arabia dunescapes

are found across the island, southeast of Detroit Harbor along South Shore Drive at **Sand Dunes Public Beach.**

Parks

The generally gravelly shoreline is rimmed with parks and beaches: **Schoolhouse Beach** in Washington Harbor, with tough and chilly swimming in a secluded setting (and extraordinarily smooth stone!); the Ridges in Jackson Harbor; and **Percy Johnson Park** on the eastern side at the tip of Lakeview Road, offering vistas of Hog Island and a nesting sanctuary. None allow camping.

Inland is where you'll find the two interesting parks. A small picnic area and park is adjacent to the airport, of all places, and people head out with a lunchtime sandwich to watch the odd plane arrival. To get there, take Main Road north, then Town Line Road east to Airport Road. The most commanding views of all are at the 200-foot heights of **Mountain Park Lookout,** just about the geometric center of the island.

Entertainment

The **Red Barn,** south of Gislason Beach along South Shore Drive, features a regular assortment of local talent—musicians or whoever else can be drummed up. The **Art and Nature Center** (1799 Main Rd., 920/847-2025) offers a weeklong midsummer music festival during which concerts and programs are offered.

RECREATION

With 75 miles of paved roadway, Washington Island was made for biking. A weekend here is just about enough time to spin around the main perimeter and nose off on a few side roads. Much of the eastern littoral roadway is gravel, as is the main artery, Michigan Road, in the center of the island. Bikes can be rented at a couple of places at the ferry dock, and trails are marked by green signs.

Field Wood Farms (one-half mile west of Main Rd. on W. Harbor Rd., 920/847-2490) offers trail rides on descendants of original Icelandic stock horses—a rarity

anywhere—and the oldest registered herd in the United States. Pony rides, riding instruction, and horse-drawn wagon rides are also available by appointment.

Fishing for 30-pound salmon is not unheard of in the sheltered waters around the island's bays; other big takes include perch, smallmouth black bass, rock bass, and especially northern pike, right in Detroit Harbor. A number of charter operations run about, including salmon and bass charters.

ACCOMMODATIONS

Washington Island features a patchwork of lodging options, stemming from its isolation. You'll find basic motels, intriguing and microscopic kiosk-cottages, spacious but threadbare cabins that look like deer-hunting shacks heated with oil furnaces, even the odd resident's spare bedroom. Finding a cheap room (as in under $100) is generally no problem. For a blast from the past, and a really cheap sleep, there's **Gibson's West Harbor Resort & Cottages** (920/847-2225, gibsonwh@itol. com, $30 s, $40 d), about halfway up the west shore from the ferry landing. Yep, they've got basic housekeeping cottages ($90 average), but the coolest of all are the sleeping rooms—tiny but tidy—with shared bathrooms above the main building, an erstwhile logging boarding house; it's all of $30 for a single and $40 for double—they even have a five-person room for $65. Absolutely nothing like it elsewhere these days.

A slight step up, the **Sunset Resort** (Old W. Harbor Rd., 920/847-2531, www.sunsetresortwi.com, $75) is a longstanding island getaway, run by the fifth generation of the inn's original Norwegian (1902) founding family. Cupped by spinneys of pine, the inn offers knotty pine cottages and one super loft cabin. Rooms are simple but clean; impromptu campfires typify the family atmosphere. Breakfasts here are legendary.

North up the road from the ferry landing at the mouth of the harbor is another smattering of no-frills accommodations, restaurants, and services. The best-known lodging here is

something that has put the island squarely on the map for those searching for something a bit different. The **◖ Washington Hotel, Restaurant, and Culinary School** (Range Line Rd., 920/847-2169, www.thewashingtonhotel.com, $125–280) is more a retreat than a lodging option. This renovated 19th-century hotel features amazing touches such as organic linens and handmade beds. Some rooms even share baths with chuffing steam showers. How about breakfast baked in an old-fashioned brick oven? Even better is the food—simply, simply worth every mile of the drive or boat to get here. Such positive feedback came from delighted lodgers that the restaurant is also a culinary academy! And rarely will you find proprietors who will work as conscientiously or heroically to solve what has caused someone to be less than happy (not me, but I've seen it and it was real-deal, not obsequious). That said, at times the hotel is booked with events and so closed to tourists, so phone or email ahead!

FOOD AND DRINK

Food for the obvious reasons, drink because you'll hear quite a bit about the potent "bitters"—an antifreeze-proof Scandinavian tradition still served in local pubs. If you can stomach a shot, you're in the club.

An island delicacy is a "lawyer." No, not the counselors, but rather another name for the burbot, a mud-dwelling gadid fish with barbels on the chin.

To-live-for Icelandic pancakes and Norwegian *barkram pankaka*—cherry and cream filled pleasures—are the house specialties at breakfast at **Sunset Resort** (Old W. Harbor Rd., 920/847-2531, 8–11 A.M. daily July–Aug., Sat.–Sun. only June and Sept., $2–7). This local hot spot serves morning grub, including homemade breads.

Landmark **Bitter's Pub and Restaurant** (Main Rd., 920/847-2496) is in Nelson's Hall, a century-old structure in the center of the island. Famed for its Bitter's Club, initiated in 1899, it draws about 10,000 visitors annually. Bitter's is the best elbow-rubbing option on the

island; the restaurant is classic Americana—steaks, seafood, and chicken. A $5 breakfast buffet, lunch, and dinner are served daily. Fish boils are held three days per week.

INFORMATION

The Washington Island Chamber of Commerce (920/847-2179, washingtonislandwi.com or washingtonislandchamber.com) has all the information you might want; it often has folks to greet you on the mainland side.

GETTING THERE AND AROUND
Getting There

Ferry lines run to and from Washington Island via the "top of the thumb." Ferries have made the seven-mile crossing somewhat quotidian, but it wasn't always so. Winter crossings used to be made by horse-drawn sleigh or—unimaginably—car, but weather conditions could change the ice or eliminate it altogether within a relatively short period. Today the ice freezes the crossing nearly solid for just more than 100 days each year, but modern ferries can take much of the ice thrown at them. When ice floes pile up during extreme cold, the ferries either "back up" and try to make an end run, or "back down" and run right at the ice. At those times, ferry service is preciously light and reservations are necessary to cross with an automobile.

You could theoretically paddle a sea kayak from Northport all the way to Washington Island—and it has been done. The lunatic fringe aspect of that notwithstanding, it would be the most breathtaking way to meet the Porte des Mortes head on. Obviously, you'd better be a damn good—and experienced—paddler.

On Island

If you've come over sans car, **Dor Cros Inn** (1922 Lobdell Point Rd., 920/847-2126) has bikes for rent; problem is, you'll have to hoof about a mile-and-a-half north up the road to get there.

A few tours/shuttles depart from the ferry dock regularly, linking with the ferries from

Northport and Gills Rock. Lots of folks rave about the **Cherry Train** (920/847-2039, www. cherrytraintours.com, $15), essentially a Chevy Suburban pulling carriages, which offers four tours daily.

Or rent your own moped for $90 per day at **Annie's** (920/854-2972) at the Island Clipper Dock.

Head up Main Road from the ferry dock to **Bread & Water Bakery & Café** (1275 Main Rd., 920/847-2400, breadandH2O@gmail. com) where they have great food, but more, where, as they say, "Kayak is spoken." Yup, the island has great kayaking, and this is your place to find a guide, a rental, or both.

◖ ROCK ISLAND STATE PARK

Less than a mile from Washington Island's Jackson Harbor as the crow flies is one man's feudal estate-turned-overgrown state park. Getting to Rock Island (920/847-2235), the most isolated state park in Wisconsin's system, necessitates not one but two ferry rides. When you get there, you've got a magnificent retreat: a small island, yes, but with delicious solitude, icy but gorgeous beaches, and the loveliest skies in Wisconsin, stars and sunrises-wise.

Native Americans lived in sporadic encampments along the island's south shore from 600 B.C. until the start of the 17th century. In approximately 1640, Potawatomi Indians migrated here from Michigan; allied Ottaway, Petun, and Hurons fleeing extermination at the hands of the Iroquois nations followed in the 1650s. The Potawatomi were visited in 1679 by Rene Robert Covelier, Sieur de la Salle, whose men built two houses, the remains of which are still visible amid the weed-choked brambles off the beach. Eventually, the French and the Potawatomi returned, establishing a trading post that lasted until 1730. Until the turn of the 20th century, the island was alternately a base camp for fishers and the site of a solitary sawmill. Rock Island is thus arguably the true "door" to Wisconsin, and a ready-made one at that—the first rock on the way across the temperamental lake from Mackinac Island.

Flora and Fauna

Here's why the isolated island is so great—no ticks, no pesky raccoons, no skunks, and no bears. In short, no perils for backpackers. The worst thing out there are the rather pernicious fields of poison ivy (though these are usually well marked). There are white-tailed deer, lemmings, foxes, and a few other small mammals and amphibians. Plenty of nonpoisonous snakes can also be seen.

The northern hardwood forest is dominated by sugar maple and American beech. The eastern hemlock is gone. The perimeters have arbor vitae (white cedar) and small varieties of red maple and red and white pine.

Sights

Two of the most historically significant buildings in Wisconsin, as deemed by the Department of the Interior, are Thordarson's massive limestone **Viking Hall** and **boathouse.** Patterned after historic Icelandic manors, the structures were cut, slab by slab, from Rock Island limestone by Icelandic artisans and workmen ferried over from Washington Island. Only the roof tiling isn't made from island material. That's a lot of rock, considering that the hall could hold more than 120 people. The hand-carved furniture, mullioned windows, and rosemaling-like detail, including runic inscriptions outlining Norse mythology, are magnificent.

The original name of Rock Island was Potawatomi Island, a name that lives on in one of the original lighthouses in Wisconsin, **Potawatomi Light,** built in 1836. The original structure was swept from the cliffs by the surly lake soon after being built but was replaced. Unfortunately, it's not open to the public except for ranger-led tours. The house is accessible via a two-hour trail.

On the east side of the island are the remnants of a former fishing village and a historic water tower—don't laugh—it, too, is on the National Register of Historic Places. The village dwelling foundations lie in the midst of thickets and are tough to spot; there are also a few cemeteries not far from the campsites.

THE MAN OF THE ROCK

In 1910, Milwaukee inventor Chester H. Thordarson plunked down $5,725 for 775-acre Rock Island. In the next 55 years, Thordarson gradually tamed the wilds and carefully transformed at least part of the island into his own private retreat.

Thordarson initially restored a few squat settlers' cabins while he pondered his masterpieces – a boathouse hewn meticulously from island limestone and, later, his grand mansion (it was never built), as well as gardens and other experiments in horticulture.

This was no simple exercise in a rich man's indulgence. As prescient as he was entrepreneurial (he made his fortune inventing more than 100 patentable devices), Thordarson developed only 30 acres of the island, with the full intent of leaving the remaining 745 as an experiment in ecological preservation. With a profound knowledge of the natural world, much of it the result of self-educated sweat, he spent the rest of his days analyzing the biological minutiae of his island. Because of this, in 1929 the University of Wisconsin gave him an honorary Master of Arts degree. The school also purchased his entire island library, containing one of the world's greatest collections of Scandinavian literature.

These are the resting spots of the children and families of lighthouse keepers and even Chief Chip-Pa-Ny, a Menominee leader.

Otherwise, the best thing to do is just skirt the shoreline and discover lake views from atop the bluffs, alternating at points with up to half a mile of sandy beach or sand dunes. Near campsite 15, you'll pass some carvings etched into the bluff, done by Thordarson's bored workers.

Recreation

At one time a sawmill buzzed the logs taken from the island; the wheel-rutted paths to the mill turned into rough roads. Thordarson let them grow over during his tenure on the island, but today they form the basis for a few miles of the park's 9.5 total hiking miles. The island is only 900-plus acres, so you've got plenty of time to cover everything, assuming you're not just spending an afternoon. If that's the case, you can do double-time and cover the perimeter in just under three hours. You'll see all the major sights and an additional magnificent view on the northeast side—on a clear day you can see all the way to Michigan's Upper Peninsula. For those less aerobically inclined, just head for the **Algonquin Nature Trail Loop,** an hour-long (maximum) traipse.

No wheeled vehicles are allowed in the park.

The dock does allow private mooring for a fee of $1 per foot.

Camping

The camping at Rock Island is absolutely splendid (next to the Apostle Islands, the best in the state), with sites strung along a beachfront of sand and, closer to the pier, large stones. Many of the sites farthest from the main compound are fully isolated, almost scooped into dunes and, thus, fully protected from wind but with smashing views (site 13 is a favorite). The island holds 40 primitive campsites (all reservable) with water and pit toilets: 35 to the southwest of the ferry landing, another 5 spread along the shore farther southeast—these are isolated backpacker sites. Two additional group campsites are also available. Reservations are a good idea in summer and fall (and essential on weekends during those times).

Note: The park is a pack-in, pack-out facility, so plan wisely.

Access

If you're not sea kayaking over, the **Karfi** (it means "seaworthy for coastal journeys" in Icelandic, so fear not; 920/847-2252) has regular service. Boats depart Jackson Harbor on Washington Island daily May 25–mid-October (usually Columbus Day for some reason); the boat leaves hourly 10 A.M.–4 P.M. in high season (June–Aug.) with an extra trip at 6 P.M. Friday. Round-trip tickets cost $9 adults and $11 campers with gear. In the off-season, you can arrange a boat, but it's prohibitively expensive.

Private boats are permitted to dock at the pier, but a mooring fee is charged.

OTHER ISLANDS
Plum and Pilot Islands

Before the establishment of the lighthouse on Plum Island, more than 100 ships were pounded into the shoals of the Door. In one year alone, Plum Island became the cemetery for 30 ships. Though safer than any U.S. highway today, it will never be sweat-free; as recently as 1989 a ship was thrown aground by the currents. The U.S. Lighthouse Service established the **Pilot Island Lighthouse** in 1858. It stands atop what an early guidebook described as "little more than a rock in the heavy-pounding seas." Two brick structures stand on Pilot Island and are about the only things still visible. Once-dense vegetation has been nearly killed off, turned into a rocky field by the ubiquitous and odoriferous droppings of federally protected cormorants, which long ago found the island and stuck around.

Plum Island had to wait until 1897 to get its imposing 65-foot skeletal steel light, after which the mortality rate within the Door dropped significantly. Plum Island—so-called for its plumb-center position in the straits—is home to an abandoned Coast Guard building on the northeast side, an old foghorn building on the southwest tip, and yet another decaying Cape Cod–style lightkeeper's residence near the range lights.

Neither island is accessible—unless your sea kayak runs into trouble—except for boat tours given during the Festival of Blossoms, usually offered three times daily from Gills Rock.

Detroit Island

Steaming into Detroit Harbor on Washington Island, look to the starboard side. The island with the crab-claw bay is Detroit Island, one of the largest satellite islands surrounding Washington Island. Settlers built the first permanent structures on the island in the early 1830s and gradually forced the displacement of the resident Ottawa and Huron Indians, who had been there for generations. Once the island was an archaeological gem, but thieves have laid waste to it. Today it is privately owned and not accessible.

GATEWAY TO DOOR COUNTY: EAST-CENTRAL WATERS

Forsaken by travelers winging to the north woods or the Door Peninsula, the East-Central Waters region is, surprisingly to many, the most historically significant region of Wisconsin. The initial and one of the most important doorways to the state later became the site of the first permanent settlements and the state's timber-and-water commercial nucleus.

When the Portage Canal linking the Upper Fox and Lower Wisconsin Rivers was completed, two of the most crucial waterways in the Great Lakes system were finally joined, allowing transport from the Atlantic Ocean all the way to the Gulf of Mexico. (The Fox River is one of the few rivers in North America to flow north.) The Fox River engineering was no mean feat for the time—it required 26 locks and dams to corral the rapids and negotiate a 200-foot drop. Within a century, though, the decrepit condition of the Fox River locks in Kaukauna earned them the distinction of being one of the 10 most endangered historic sites.

Thus, Wisconsin established the **Fox-Wisconsin Riverways Heritage Corridor** to preserve what was left. The entire length of the Fox River is being eyed by the National Park Service as a National Heritage Corridor. In addition to the locks, some of the only extant French-style agricultural developments can still be seen—they're recognizable by their long, narrow drawbacks from the river, as opposed to the usual patchwork parallelograms of the other European immigrants.

© THOMAS HUHTI

HIGHLIGHTS

◖ **Kohler:** An erstwhile corporate employee town, the state's most reputed (if not astonishing) resort is also here (page 61).

◖ **Wisconsin Maritime Museum:** Learn about everything from wooden schooners to WWII submaking at this wowser (page 66).

◖ **Point Beach State Forest:** Relax along a grand littoral stretch and amid ecological precious zones (page 69).

◖ **The Pack:** 'Nuff said (page 70).

◖ **The History Museum at the Castle and A.K.A. Houdini:** Learn the secrets of Harry Houdini's escape tricks (page 81).

◖ **High Cliff State Park:** It's worth a stop for its magnificent perch above Lake Winnebago (page 86).

◖ **EAA Air Adventure Museum and Fly-In Convention:** The museum is fabulous; the convention is jaw-drop kid-in-all-of-us amazing (page 89)!

◖ **The Little White Schoolhouse:** Donkey-blue Wisconsin founded the elephant party, believe it or not (page 95).

◖ **Wolf River:** This natural beauty features dells, rapids, misty cascades, all surrounded by depths of public lands (page 100).

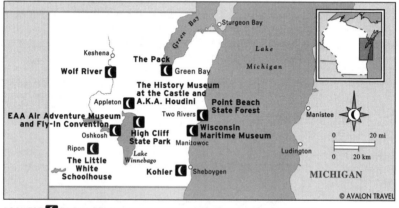

LOOK FOR ◖ TO FIND RECOMMENDED SIGHTS, ACTIVITIES, DINING, AND LODGING.

HISTORY

Early nomadic Paleo-Indians arrived as the glaciers retreated; this was well before Jean Nicolet came calling in 1634. The Jesuits thereafter attempted to found the westernmost fringe community of New France. Later, immigrants began pouring in, harvesting the timber treasures for the rapacious needs of a burgeoning nation. For a while, with the hinterlands timber industry and the prodigious fishing harvests and shipping receipts, this was the richest section of the state.

Though the timber has slowed to a less heady trickle and the shipbuilding and fishing fleets are mostly gone, the region still juxtaposes some great recreation with the zenith of Wisconsin's early economic triumvirate.

PLANNING YOUR TIME

A weekend is out of the question, unless you center yourself somewhere in the historic **Fox Cities** area and pick and choose—by region or activity. Otherwise, you could spend a night and day in either Oshkosh or Appleton and

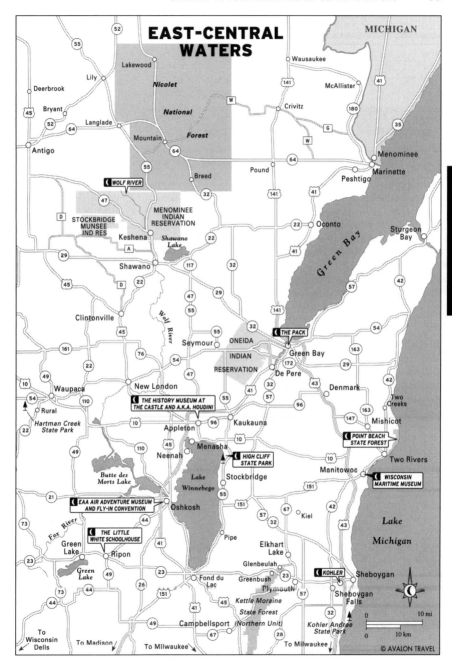

EAST-CENTRAL WATERS

then spend the second in any of the following: Oshkosh (EAA Air Adventure Museum) and Ripon (Birthplace of the Republican Party); High Cliff State Park to Kohler/Sheboygan; the Wolf River; or Manitowoc (Wisconsin Maritime Museum) and Two Rivers (Point Beach State Forest). This author would just spend the whole two days salivating over Packerdom at Lambeau Field in Green Bay . . .

Sheboygan

Sheboygan has come a long way, touristically speaking. This phlegmatic, gritty industrial town was once anything but a must-see.

Fast-forward two decades. Herculean efforts and millions of dollars have made possible the renovation of marinas, promenades, lighted walkways, bike trails, building facades, and harbor breakwaters. It's almost nearing postcard cliché realms.

(Progress? Well, *Reader's Digest* once named Sheboygan the number one "Family Friendly" city in the United States.)

Sheboygan has never lacked fame for one other thing: bratwurst. It's the self-proclaimed Bratwurst Capital of the World and nobody touches Sheboyganites and their brats. Innumerable neighborhood butchers still turn out family-secret-recipe bratwurst (everyone is slobberingly devoted to his or her own butcher), and Brat Days (www.bratdays.org) in summer is one of Wisconsin's largest food festivals.

History

Nearby cascades inspired the Ojibwa name Shaw-bwah-way-gun, "the sound like the wind of the rushing waters." Due to its fortuitous location, equidistant from Milwaukee and Manitowoc, the village erected one of the first decent piers along Lake Michigan, allowing lake schooners and ferries to bring tens of thousands of German, Dutch, and English immigrants, many dairy farmers, to town.

During the final wave of German immigration, between 1880 and 1890, some areas hereabouts were (and are) 95 percent German. Most of the immigrants were woodworkers, so several furniture and wood-product factories

opened. Thus, Sheboygan also became known as the city of cheese and chairs.

SIGHTS
John Michael Kohler Arts Center

This superlative arts center (608 New York Ave., 920/458-6144, www.jmkac.org, 10 A.M.–5 P.M. Mon.–Fri., also till 8 P.M. Tues. and Thurs., 10 A.M.–4 P.M. Sat.–Sun., free) is one of Sheboygan's cultural landmarks. The wondrously progressive, eclectic grouping of galleries is devoted to contemporary art in all media, including galleries devoted to self-taught artists. The center has been nationally recognized for its unusually broad scope and its efforts to

Sheboygan's distinctive lighthouse

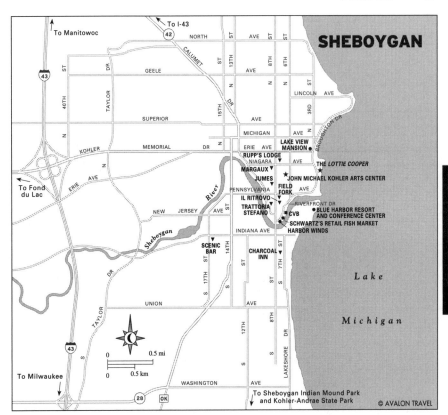

incorporate the community—no PR-speak, it means *the whole community*—in its undertakings. This explains its consistent ratings by industry groups in the top 10 nationwide.

The Boardwalk

The city center's gem is this winding walkway alongside the Sheboygan River and Riverfront Drive, trailing gentrification as it goes. The old fishing shanties have been transformed into antique shops, art galleries, restaurants, and other retail outlets. A few old weatherbeaten shacks remain.

The *Lottie Cooper*

One of 62 wrecks near Sheboygan, the *Lottie Cooper,* a three-masted lumber schooner, went

down in a gale off Sheboygan on April 9, 1894, killing one. Including one of the longest salvaged keels of a Great Lakes wreck, the vessel now rests in Deland Park, near the North Pier. It's along a lovely lakefront promenade.

Sheboygan Indian Mound Park

An archaic relic (5000 S. 9th St., 920/459-3444, free) along the Black River region in south Sheboygan, this place is eerily impressive. The 18 Native American effigy mounds, in myriad geometric and animal shapes, date from A.D. 500. A beautiful nature trail runs along a creek.

Kohler-Andrae State Park

A personal favorite, this may well be the best stretch of beach along Wisconsin's Lake

Kohler-Andrae State Park near Sheboygan

Michigan shoreline (1020 Beach Park Ln., 920/451-4080). It includes two miles of wind-swept beach and a plank trail that meanders through the fragile Kohler Dunes Natural Area, one of the state's rarest habitats (an interdunal wetland). I've never *not* stumbled across white-tailed deer among the dunes. The chilly waters off the park are home to about 50 shipwrecks (a diver's paradise). Many of the recovered wrecks are on display at the Sanderling Center here.

Henning's Wisconsin Cheese

Nobody makes 'em anymore like they do at the too-cool Henning's Wisconsin Cheese (20201 Point Creek Rd., Kiel, 920/894-3022, www.henningscheese.com, 7 A.M.–4 P.M. Mon.–Fri., 8 A.M.–noon Sat.), northeast of Sheboygan in little Kiel. The operation is enormous enough, complete with an outstanding museum of cheese-making. You'll snap lots of images on your mobile phone of the gigantic 12,000-pound wheels of cheddar cheese, this being the only remaining place in the United States to make 'em!

RECREATION
Charter Fishing

Sheboygan's 300-slip **Harbor Centre Marina** (821 Broughton Dr., 920/458-6665) offers great fishing with about 35 licensed skippers operating out of Sheboygan. Prices vary, but it's generally around $300–450 (not including tip or a Wisconsin fishing license) for 1–4 people for a half-day charter; some outfits offer minicharters.

Old Plank Road Trail

In 1843, the territorial legislature, hoping to effect permanent settlement in today's Sheboygan County region, began building the first plank road to reach all the way to Fond du Lac. It was completed in 1852. Today, the Old Plank Road Trail is a paved 17-mile-long multipurpose recreation trail running from western Sheboygan to Greenbush and the Kettle Moraine State Forest's northern unit (and thus the Ice Age Trail), via Kohler and Plymouth, a lovely ride in spots.

BRATWURST: THE WISCONSIN DISH

Bratwurst, a Germanic legacy of Wisconsin, is the unofficial state dish. The brat (pronounced to rhyme with "plot," not "splat!") is pervasive here. Supermarkets devote entire lengths of freezers to accommodate sausage-makers. Many towns still have old butcher shops that string up homemade flavors.

THE IMMIGRANT EPICURE

Strictly speaking, the bratwurst is but one of hundreds of varieties of sausage, according to official (and draconian) German food law. Actually, sausage-making was here with the Native Americans, who had long stuffed deer intestines and hides with wild rice, grains, meats, offal, and herbs to produce pemmican, which is, technically, a sausage.

From the earliest settlement of the state, immigrants did make their own sausage. Wisconsin's bratwurst, unlike some varieties, is almost strictly made from pork. The internal mixtures would consist of meat, fat, and seasonings, along with occasional starches such as rice and bread. Concoctions were and are highly secret – similar to the recipe for Coca-Cola.

INFINITE VARIETIES

The main categories of Wisconsin sausage follow. In addition, the Czech method includes a rice sausage and head cheese; the Norwegians make *sylte*, which is spiced and salted in brine.

German: There are a zillion kinds of German sausage. Bratwurst are most often seasoned with marjoram, pepper, salt, caraway, and nutmeg.

Italian: Italian sausage is sweeter and hotter. Fennel gives it its trademark flavor.

Polish: Think garlic-heavy ring of two-inch-thick, dark pink bologna-esque sausage is traditionally steam-fried for dinner (and then cut into sandwiches for leftovers and lunchboxes). Polish recipes often call for red cabbage and mustard sauces.

BRATS IN SHEBOYGAN

The place to go is **Miesfeld's Triangle Market** (4811 Venture Dr., two blocks north of the intersection of I-43 and WI 42, 414/565-6328), where Chuck and the gang have been putting out national-award-winning sausages (15 varieties of bratwurst have thus far garnered 68 national awards) for as long as anybody can remember. The town has a celebratory fit of indulgent mayhem come August with its Bratwurst Days.

Some brat-related Sheboygan-only tips:

- "double" – you simply cannot eat just one brat

- "fryer" – whatever thing you cook the brat on (Cheeseheads otherwise say "grill")

- "fry out" – used as both a noun and a verb

- "hard roll" – it looks like a hamburger bun but it's bigger and harder (sometimes called sennel roll)

PREPARATION

Microwave a brat and you'll incur the wrath of any Wisconsinite. Frying one is OK, but traditionally a brat must be grilled. Brats work best if you parboil them in beer and onions for 10-15 minutes before putting them on the grill. Sheboyganites absolutely cringe at parboiling, so don't tell them I told you. Another no-no is roughage crammed in the bun – lettuce, tomatoes, and so on; even sauerkraut, loved by Milwaukeeans, is barely tolerated by Sheboyganites.

Another option: Parboil brats briefly. Sear in butter in a frying pan. Set aside. Pour two cups dark beer into fry pan and scrape residue. Combine a finely chopped onion, some beef stock, juice from one lemon, and maybe one chopped green pepper. Put brats back in and boil 12-15 minutes. Remove brats and place on hot grill. Sauce can be thickened with flour or cornstarch and poured over the top. A Cheesehead will stick the sauce in a bun alongside the brat with mustard.

EAST-CENTRAL WATERS

ACCOMMODATIONS

Nothing is cheap in Sheboygan, if you can even find a place; Sheboygan for some reason lacks myriad motels—and enough nearby camping. Best bet would be east of I-43 at nearly every exit.

The **Harbor Winds** (905 S. 8th St., 920/452-9000, www.pridehospitality.com, $79) is the only place on the water in Sheboygan. An observation deck affords a great view, the staff is friendly, and residents get a free morning newspaper and breakfast.

The **Blue Harbor Resort and Conference Center** (725 Blue Harbor Dr., 920/452-2900, www.blueharborresort.com, $229–689) is a four-level Victorian replica with an indoor water park. The self-enclosed place boasts spas, fitness centers, two enormous restaurants, arcades, and more.

With a commanding view above Lake Michigan is the **Lake View Mansion** (303 St. Clair St., 920/457-5253, www.lakeviewmansion.com, $159–249), a gorgeous historic structure. The five rooms all have private baths and a view of the lake.

FOOD
Brats

To sample the "best of the wurst" (they say, not me!)—you've got myriad options. For me, it's the **Charcoal Inn** (1313 S. 8th St., 920/458-6988, 6 A.M.–9 P.M. Tues.–Fri., 6 A.M.–7 P.M. Sat., and 1637 Greele Ave., 920/458-1147, 5 A.M.–7 P.M. Tues.–Sat., $4–8), where they still fire up a fryer every morning to supplement its unpretentious Midwest fare.

Fish Fries

The **Scenic Bar** (1635 Indiana Ave., 920/452-2881, 4–9 P.M. Tues.–Thurs. and Sat., 11 A.M.–2 P.M. and 3:30–10 P.M. Fri., 4–8 P.M. Sun., $5) has standard supper-club-in-a-tavern fare, with a fish fry Friday at noon and night (pike, bluegill and perch in addition to standard cod). Most locals point this place out as the place for unpretentious fare.

It's takeout only at **Schwarz's Retail Fish Market** (828 Riverfront Dr., 920/452-0576), the best place in town for fresh fish.

American

Jumes (504 N. 8th St., 920/452-4914, 6 A.M.–7:30 P.M. daily, $3 and up), a retro diner, is the place to go to rub shoulders with the locals, read the compendious menu, and enjoy the dirt-cheap heart-stopping breakfast. My Sheboyganite friends swear by this one.

Margaux (821 N. 8th St., 920/457-6565, 11:30 A.M.–1:30 P.M. Tues.–Fri., 5–9 P.M. Mon.–Sat., $8–18) is a casually upscale place for pan-world cuisine and the spot to get away from the red-meat-heavy fare of these parts.

Enjoy rib-sticking American food at **Rupp's Lodge** (925 N. 8th St., 920/459-8155, 11 A.M.–2 P.M. and 5–9 P.M. Mon.–Fri., 4–9 P.M. Sat.–Sun., $5–25), which has been around for six decades. Aged, hand-cut steaks are the specialty here, along with standard supper club fare. Through a glass partition, you get to watch the food being prepared in the kitchen. On Friday and Saturday nights, patrons join in singalongs at a piano.

Italian

Dishing up the best Italian is the ever-friendly **Trattoria Stefano** (522 S. 8th St., 920/452-8455, 5–9 P.M. Mon.–Thurs., 5–10 P.M. Fri.–Sat., $12–28), a casually upscale place with a bright pastel (and handmade brick) environment. For years a foodie must-stop, comments from readers have begun to mention a bit of a dip here. Hopefully it's an aberration. BTW, for a more subdued Italian experience, across the street is another of the owner's ventures: **Il Ritrovo** (515 S. 8th St., 920/803-7516, lunch and dinner Mon.–Sat.), dinner with pizza good enough for Naples' authorities to have certified it as OK! If that weren't enough, Stefano has also opened **Field to Fork** (511 S. 8th St., 920/694-0322, 7 A.M.–3 P.M. Mon.–Sat.) next door to the pizzeria—think locavore deli and light lunch place (love the coney dog!).

INFORMATION

The **Sheboygan County Convention and Visitors Bureau** (712 Riverfront Dr., Ste. 101, 920/457-9497 or 800/457-9497, www.visitsheboygan.com) is along the Boardwalk.

GETTING AROUND

If the city budget allows, Sheboygan has a quaint, battery-propelled replica **trolley** that buzzes about the downtown area during summer.

Vicinity of Sheboygan

◖ KOHLER

A planned workers' community surrounding the operations of the Kohler Company, Kohler is trim and attractive—thoroughly inspiring for a sense of community. Kohler also houses the state's most incredible resort/restaurant and puts on unforgettable factory tours.

Sights

The **Kohler Factory** and, to a lesser extent, **Kohler Design Center** (101 Upper Rd., 920/457-3699, www.kohler.com, 8 A.M.–5 P.M. Mon.–Fri., 10 A.M.–4 P.M. Sat.–Sun. and holidays, free) are must-sees. The international manufacturer of bathroom fixtures here showcases in its 2.5-hour tour the company's early factory and factory-town history, along with its wares in an incredible "Great Wall of China." Also featured are a theater, ceramic art gallery, and more. Tours of the factory itself are on weekdays only and require advance registration.

Waelderhaus (House in the Woods) (1100 W. Riverside Dr., 920/452-4079, tours 2, 3, and 4 P.M. hourly, free), a dwelling based on homes from the mountainous Austrian Bregenzerwald region commissioned by a daughter of the Kohler founder, contains antique furnishings and highlights such as candle-reflected water-globe lighting.

Hands down the best golf in Wisconsin—and some say the Midwest—is found in Kohler at the **American Club** resort (Highland Dr., 920/457-8000, www.destinationkohler.com). **Blackwolf Run** offers two PGA championship courses—one of them was the highest-rated gold medal course in the United States according to *Golf* magazine. Newer are the preternaturally lovely courses of **Whistling Straits,** designed to favor the old seaside links courses of Britain; it's even got sheep wandering about! There are the Straits Course and a challenging Dunes Course, both PGA championship courses. In 2000 Whistling Straits unveiled its new Irish Course, a companion course to the first Straits course; among other things it features some of the tallest sand dunes in the United States. It's all good enough for the PGA Championship to have been played here—twice. Call 920/457-4446 for details; it's neither cheap nor easy to golf these courses.

Accommodations and Food

Easily Wisconsin's most breathtaking resort, ◖ **The American Club** (Highland Dr., 920/457-8000, www.destinationkohler.com, $260–1,210) is the Midwest's only AAA five-diamond resort. The 1918 red brick facade of an erstwhile workers' hostel and dormitory has been retained, along with the original carriage house, though both have been poshly retrofitted. A full slate of recreation is offered, of note two championship Pete Dye golf courses (one of them considered one of the most perfect examples in the world of a shot-master's course). There's also a private 500-acre wildlife preserve to explore. If that's not enough, the seven dining rooms and restaurants include the state's best—the Immigrant Room, winner of the prestigious DiRoNa Award. Here, various rooms offer the ethnic cuisine and heritage of France, Holland, Germany, Scandinavia, and England. The food is created with regional Wisconsin ingredients. Jackets are required.

If ever you splurge in Wisconsin, this is one of the places to do it; if not, consider the tours offered Monday–Saturday at 2 P.M. for a look-see.

SHEBOYGAN FALLS

Sheboygan actually got its start near these somewhat thundering falls of the Sheboygan River. The town has a great riverwalk with views of the falls and two very historic districts. Among the grandest bed-and-breakfasts in the area is (**The Rochester Inn** (504 Water St., 920/467-3123 or 800/421-4667, $109 s or d), a massive 1848 general store. The rooms all have parlors with wingback lounges, and there are four split-level luxury suites and a grand internal spiral staircase.

Richard's (501 Monroe St., 920/467-6401, lunch Tues. only, dinner Mon.–Sat., $6–35), in an 1840s stagecoach inn, features excellent finer dining.

PLYMOUTH

Plymouth lies just west of Sheboygan and would definitely be on a National Register of Quaint Places—the aesthetics of its early Yankee settlements remain amazingly intact. Initially a solitary tavern-cum-stage stop, as all rail traffic passed through the little burg, it eventually became the center of the cheese industry in eastern Wisconsin (the first Cheese Exchange was here).

Sights

The local chamber of commerce has an impressively mapped and detailed historical and architectural walking tour highlighting about 50 buildings. The visitors center is itself an architectural highlight: the **Plymouth Center** (E. Mill St., 920/893-0079, 10 A.M.–2 P.M. Sun.–Thurs.), a restored 1920s edifice that also houses a historical museum and art galleries.

Accommodations and Food

Historic bed-and-breakfasts are everywhere you turn. A structure woodworkers will want to see is the **52 Stafford Irish Guest House** (52 Stafford St., 920/893-0552, www.52stafford. com, $100). The 19 guest rooms are decent, but the main attraction here is the food. The limited but ambitious menu changes a lot; the signature meal is an Irish beef brisket basted in Guinness—it'll wow you. The rich woods, ornate stained glass, and original fixtures give the place a special atmosphere. Do drop by Wednesday evenings for rousing Irish music.

ELKHART LAKE

Northwest of Sheboygan is one of the region's first resort areas (www.elkhartlake.com). In the early 20th century, well-to-do Chicagoans sought out the quiet getaway and, later, so did high-profile mobsters such as John Dillinger. Another major draw is the international speedway **Road America,** North America's longest natural road-racing course. (And a couple of, um, subdued local museums.)

Accommodations and Food

One of the oldest and most established lodgings (family-run since 1916) is **Siebkens** (284 S. Lake St., 920/876-2600, www.siebkens. com, $139–459 weekends), a turn-of-the-20th-century resort with two white-trimmed main buildings (open only in summer) and a year-round lake cottage. A nod to modernity in their plush new condos is also available. The classic tavern and dining room serve up regional fare on an old porch.

Much posher is the (**Osthoff Resort** (101 Osthoff Ave., 920/876-3366, www.osthoff. com, $170–625), with lavish comfort and fine lake views. Lola's dining room and the Aspira spa are superb (good enough that they have a cooking school here now). This is a real *wow* experience.

One of the most extraordinary meals of late has come at the newer (**Paddock Club** (61 S. Lake St., 920/876-3288, 4 P.M.–close Tues.– Sun., closed March, $18–38). You'll find indescribably good new American cuisine in another erstwhile gangster hangout.

KETTLE MORAINE STATE FOREST-NORTHERN UNIT

A crash course in geology helps preface a trip through the 29,000 acres of the northern unit of the Kettle Moraine State Forest (262/626-2116). The northern unit was chosen as the site of the Henry Reuss Ice Age Interpretive Center—on the Ice Age National Scenic

enjoying splash time in a lake in the Kettle Moraine State Forest-Northern Unit

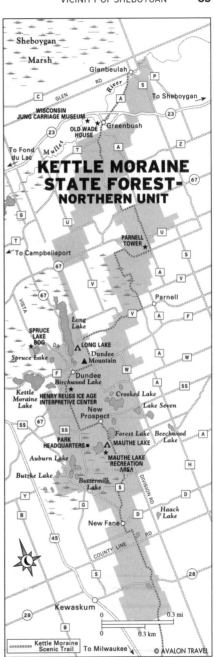

EAST-CENTRAL WATERS

Trail—given its variegated topography of kettles, terminal moraines, kames, and eskers, and all that other geological vocabulary. Surrounded by suburban expansion, it somehow manages to hold 12 State Natural Areas inside its borders.

This northern swath of forest is the complement to its sibling southwest of Milwaukee. Supporters of the forest have always envisioned the two sections of forest as a quasi-superforest, concatenate segments of lands acting as an urban buffer zone along a 120-mile eco-corridor.

Henry Reuss Ice Age Interpretive Center

Along WI 67 near the Highway G junction is the Henry Reuss Ice Age Interpretive Center (920/533-8322, 8:30 A.M.–4 P.M. Mon.–Fri. and 9:30 A.M.–5 P.M. Sat.–Sun. Apr.–Oct., shorter hours in winter). The back deck has outstanding vistas of the whole topographical shebang. The exhibits and documentary theater are well worth a stop. A self-guided

ICE AGE NATIONAL SCENIC TRAIL

Glaciation affected all of the Upper Midwest, but nowhere is it more exposed than in Wisconsin. Southwestern Wisconsin's Driftless Area is also the only purely unglaciated region on the planet surrounded by glacial till.

Wisconsin's epic Ice Age National Scenic Trail is a 1,200-mile course skirting morainic topography left behind by the state's four glacial epochs. It's also an ongoing project, started in the 1950s and still being pieced together. When county chapters have finally cobbled together enough municipal, county, and state forest land with donated private land for right-of-way, Potawatomi State Park in Door County will be linked with Interstate State Park on the St. Croix National Scenic Riverway via one continuous footpath.

THE ICE AGE SCIENTIFIC RESERVE

Technically, the trail is but a segment of the Ice Age National Scientific Reserve, established by congressional fiat in 1971 after decades of wrangling by forward-thinking ecologist Ray Zillmer of Milwaukee.

The reserve's nine units are scattered along the advance of the glacial periods and highlight their most salient residuals. Numerous other state and county parks, equally impressive geologically, fill in the gaps. Kames, eskers, drumlins, moraines, kettles, and all the glacial effects are highlighted in the units on the east side of the state. An interpretive center is planned for Cross Plains, Wisconsin, west of Madison.

THE TRAIL

As of 2010, around 700 miles of *official* trails had been established either by the National Park Ser-

vice, county chapters, or state parks; the rest are link-up trails, roads, or even Main Street USA's. The longest established stretches come in the Chequamegon and Nicolet National Forests, along the Sugar River Trail in southwest Wisconsin, through the Kettle Moraine State Forest, and along the Ahnapee State Trail in the Door Peninsula. Hiking the whole thing is possible, though it takes about three months and oodles of patience attempting to circumvent cityscapes where segments have not yet opened.

Camping is a problem along the route if you're outside an established park or forest. Do not trespass or private landowners may stop any progress.

INFORMATION

View the National Park Service's website (nps.gov/iatr) or contact the Ice Age National Scenic Trail (608/441-5610, www.iceagetrail.org) in Madison.

ICE AGE NATIONAL SCENIC TRAIL

Lake Superior

MICHIGAN

Terminal

Moraine

Age

Ice

Green Bay Lobe

Lake Michigan

Northern Kettle Moraine

MINNESOTA

Campbellsport Drumlins

National

Terminal

IOWA

Trail

Moraine

0   40 mi

0   40 km

Scenic

© AVALON TRAVEL

ILLINOIS

40-mile auto geology tour starts from the center. A short nature trail winds from the building outside.

Wade House and Jung Carriage Museum

Along WI 23 in Greenbush the **Old Wade House** (Hwy. T, 920/526-3271, 10 A.M.–5 P.M. daily mid-May–mid-Oct., $11 adults) sits along the oak plank road that stretched from Sheboygan to Fond du Lac. The state historic site is a wondrous, detailed reconstruction of the 1848 original sawmill—note the post and beam work—one of few like it in the United States. Environmentally friendly construction was used—as in the original.

Perhaps the Wade House's biggest draw is the impressive **Wisconsin Jung Carriage Museum,** with the state's largest collection of hand- and horse-drawn vehicles (many rideable).

Scenic Drives

The forest offers a smashing scenic drive. As you drive along ribbony highways (including official Rustic Roads), you'll trace the oldest geology in Wisconsin, 10,000-year-old outwash of the last glacial period.

The scenic drive is linked in the south with other great back roads all the way to the Southern Unit, about 40 miles away. It's hard to get lost; just follow the acorn-shaped road signs. From Sheboygan Marsh in the north to Whitewater Lake in the southern unit, the road totals about 120 miles and passes through six counties.

Recreation

More than 140 miles of trails snake through the forest's narrow northern unit, including the highlight, the sublime 31-mile segment of the **Ice Age National Scenic Trail.** It runs the length of the park and hooks up with five other forest trails for plenty of options. Five shelters are along the way. Backpackers must have permits (generally easy to obtain, but plan early for high season).

The best-known trail is the 11-mile **Zillmer Trail,** accessible via Highway SS; there's one tough ridge with a great vista.

Some say the best view (1,300 feet above sea level, plus 450 feet above the tower) is the one from **Parnell Tower,** two miles north of WI 67 via Highway A.

Parkview General Store (262/626-8287), north of the Mauthe Lake Recreation Area entrance, has bicycle, paddleboat, canoe, and rowboat rentals.

Camping

In all, 400 campsites are available, lots of them reservable. Primitive shelter camping is possible along the Glacial Trail. **Mauthe Lake** also has a tepee for rent.

Manitowoc and Two Rivers

These Lake Michigan quasi-sister cities were originally home to tribes of Ojibwa, Potawatomi, and Ottawa. The tranquil harbors attracted fur traders, and by 1795, the Northwest Fur Company had built its post here. Under Europeans, the area prospered during the heady early decades of whitefish plunder and shipbuilding, the latter still around.

Charter Fishing

Charter fishing is big business. Coho and king salmon, along with lake and brown trout (and some rainbow), are most popular for skippers in these waters.

MANITOWOC

This small bight was a port of call for weary Great Lakes travelers—the earliest ones in birchbark canoes—heading for Chicago. Drive out into the countryside and you can still see smokehouses and bake ovens on early farmsteads, log threshing barns large enough to drive machinery through, split-rail fencing, and unique cantilever house designs.

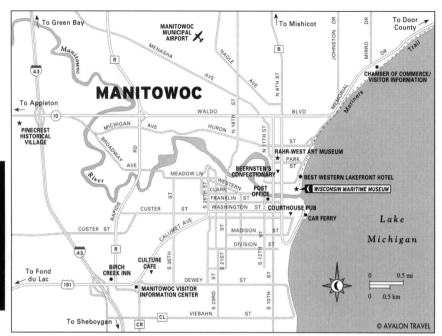

An enormous fishing industry came and, thanks to overfishing through injudicious use of drift nets and seines, went. However, the so-called Clipper City shifted to producing ships beginning in the 1800s, peaking around World War II, when Manitowoc's shipyard became one of the most important naval production facilities in the country.

C Wisconsin Maritime Museum

At peak WWII production, Manitowoc eclipsed even major east coast shipbuilding centers. Its legacy is remembered at the Wisconsin Maritime Museum (75 Maritime Dr., 920/684-0218, www.wisconsinmaritime.org, 9 A.M.–6 P.M. daily Memorial Day weekend–Labor Day weekend, until 5 P.M. the rest of the year, $12 includes access to the *Cobia*). Flanked by the USS *Cobia* submarine (a National Historic Landmark, one of 28 built here, and one reason Manitowoc is the only U.S. city with streets named after subs!), the museum is an amazing conglomeration of Great Lakes (especially local) maritime history.

Other Sights

The **Pinecrest Historical Village** (Pine Crest La., 920/684-5110, 9 A.M.–5 P.M. daily May–Oct., $6 adults) is an ensemble of more than 25 extant buildings brought here and painstakingly restored on 60 acres. Structures date from as far back as the 1840s.

The **Rahr-West Art Museum** (610 N. 8th St. at Park St., 920/683-4501, 10 A.M.–4 P.M. Mon.–Fri., till 8 P.M. Wed., 11 A.M.–4 P.M. Sat.–Sun., free) is an 1891 Victorian with intricate woodworking and grand beamed ceilings housing one of the finer collections of art in the Midwest. A tidbit: The brass ring in the street out front is where a piece of Sputnik hit in 1962.

Stretch your legs on the **Mariners Trail,** a 12-mile-long paved recreation trail between Manitowoc and Two Rivers.

© THOMAS HUHTI

USS *Cobia* standing guard over Manitowoc's harbor

Accommodations

Most motels and hotels, including several chain operations, are clustered around the I-43/U.S. 151 interchange. The **Birch Creek Inn** (4626 Calumet Ave., 920/684-3374 or 800/424-6126, www.birchcreekinn.com, $50 s or d) put $1 million in renovations to turn itself into a quaint little spot: a 1940s motor inn with a cottage complex—unique!

The luxury accommodation in town is the **Best Western Lakefront Hotel** (101 Maritime Dr., 920/682-7000 or 800/654-5353, $99), the only place right on the lake and adjacent to the maritime museum.

Food

Superb sandwiches with homemade breads and healthful insides are to be had at **Culture Cafe** (3949 Calumet Ave., 920/682-6844, $4–11).

Boisterous is the **Courthouse Pub** (1001 S. 8th St., 920/686-1166, 11 A.M.–9 P.M. Mon.–Fri., 3:30–9:30 P.M. Sat., $5–15), which handcrafts its own brews and has above-average pub grub in a painstakingly restored 1860s Greek revival.

Chocolate fanatics and the dessert-minded should not miss **Beernsten's Confectionary** (108 N. 8th St., 920/684-9616, 10 A.M.–10 P.M. daily), a renowned local chocolatier for about 50 years.

Information

The super Manitowoc Information Center (920/683-4388 or 800/627-4896, www. manitowoc.info) is prominently housed on the western highway junction and has a 24-hour kiosk.

Getting There

Originally one of seven railroad and passenger ferries plying the route between here and Ludington, Michigan, the **SS Badger** (800/841-4243, www.ssbadger.com) is a wonderful anachronism. Though it's technically a steamship—the last of its kind on Lake Michigan—you can hardly tell thanks to modern pollution controls. Crossings take four hours and depart daily mid-May–mid-October, with two departures June–late August from Manitowoc.

Round-trip fares are $109 per person, $59 per car. Some intriguing deals are available.

TWO RIVERS

Two Rivers is, they say, the fishing capital of Lake Michigan. But residents are even prouder of another claim to fame: The ice-cream sundae was invented here in 1881 at a 15th Street soda fountain. (Yes, yes, we know—it's in a friendly rivalry with another not-to-be-mentioned-here U.S. city for this honor.) The mammoth historic **Washington House Museum and Visitor Center** (17th St. and Jefferson St., 920/793-2490, 9 A.M.–9 P.M. daily May–Oct., 9 A.M.–5 P.M. daily Nov.–Apr., free), once an immigrant hotel-cum-dance hall/saloon, dispenses information as well as great ice cream at a mock-up of the original fountain that made the town famous.

Sights and Recreation

Across from Washington House is the fascinating **Woodtype/Printing Museum** (1619 Jefferson St., 920/794-6272, 9 A.M.–5 P.M.

Tues.–Sat., free), with vintage equipment for international woodtyping. The **Two Rivers History Museum** (1810 Jefferson St., 920/793-1103, 10 A.M.–4 P.M. daily, free) two blocks away was once a convent.

At **Rogers Street Fishing Village** (2102 Jackson St., 920/793-5905, 10 A.M.–4 P.M. Mon.–Fri. and noon–4 P.M. Sat.–Sun. May–Oct., $4 adults), artifacts include those from the regional U.S. Coast Guard, especially its lighthouse operations. There is a lot of shipwreck memorabilia—folks say it's Wisconsin's largest shipwreck exhibit—and plenty of retired vessels.

Excellent are the **Woodland Dunes** west 10 miles along WI 310. The eponymous spiny mounds were the littoral edges of a glacial lake.

Accommodations

Farthest south from town toward Manitowoc, the **Village Inn on the Lake** (3310 WI 42, 920/794-8818 or 800/551-4795, www.villageinnwi.com, $99) is a decent, family-run operation—a two-level motel (with RV sites) with a coffee shop and minigolf course on the premises.

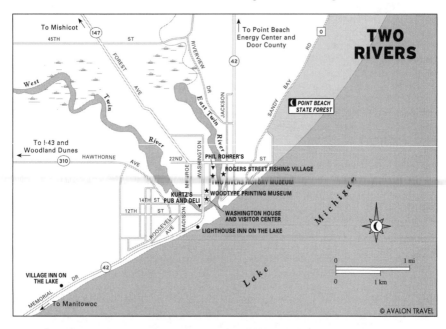

© THOMAS HUHTI

Point Beach State Forest's gorgeous lighthouse

The **Lighthouse Inn on the Lake** (1515 Memorial Dr., 920/793-4524 or 800/228-6416, $124) is showing its age but still fine. The standard rooms aren't exactly capacious, but they do have magnificent vistas of Lake Michigan—and some higher-priced rooms *are* quite large.

Food

Hole-in-the-wall ◖ **Phil Rohrer's** (1303 22nd St., 920/794-8500, 7 A.M.–8 P.M. Mon.–Sat., from under $1) serves classic diner fare. One of my personal favorites, it has a handful of swivel seats, fewer booths, and since 1962 has had some of the state's greatest "ho-made" soups with the slider burgers and rib-sticking comfort food specials. Try the raw fries.

One of the best-known restaurants in this region is **Kurtz's Pub and Deli** (1410 Washington St., 920/793-1222, 11 A.M.–10 P.M. Mon.–Sat., $4–11). It was established in 1904 to serve the rollicking sailors hopping off Great Lakes steamers and clippers. Today, let's call it an "upscale pub."

Don't forget: The dessert tray is at the visitors center!

◖ POINT BEACH STATE FOREST

Just north of Two Rivers is a gorgeous tract of state forest—Point Beach State Forest (920/794-7480), off Highway O, six miles east of town. You can't miss it: The majestic white lighthouse towers above the sandy pines. The wind-whipped 2,900 acres spread along latte-colored sandy beaches; the wicked shoals offshore have pulled plenty of ships to their graves. The lighthouse is functional, but public access is sporadic. The preserved ridges along the shoreline are residual effects of a glacial lake last seen retreating 5,500 years ago, one reason the entire forest is a State Scientific Area. One of Wisconsin's official **Rustic Roads** stretches along the park—Highway O, a.k.a. Sandy Bay Road.

Up the road farther is the **Point Beach Energy Center** (6600 Nuclear Rd., 920/755-6400, 9:30 A.M.–4 P.M. Tues.–Sat., free). The Point Beach nuclear plant has caused some controversy in Wisconsin because of plans to store waste aboveground in concrete casks. Nonetheless, the energy center features worthwhile hands-on exhibits on energy, as well as a nature trail and observation tower.

One of nine Ice Age National Scientific Reserves in Wisconsin is the **Two Creeks** area, a few miles north of here. Two Creeks contains the remnants of a 12,000-year-old buried glacial forest.

DENMARK

Also a hop off the interstate on the way to Green Bay is the Danish enclave of Denmark, known heretofore as Copenhagen. There's lots of old Danish architecture downtown, and more cheese shops per capita than anywhere else.

EAST-CENTRAL WATERS

Green Bay

La Baye

Not only colorful, *La Baye Verte* was a haven from the volatility of Lake Michigan. In 1669 New France established under Jesuit overview an official settlement—the first permanent settlement in what would be Wisconsin—at the mouth of the bay near the present-day suburb of De Pere.

The bay region's explorers and trappers found a wealth of beavers and new networks of inland waterways—meaning trees; the wilderness from here to the Fox River Valley produced more than any other region in New France.

After a century of changing hands, the bay was the transportation conduit, for both commerce and immigration, to the rest of Wisconsin and, via the Mississippi, the country.

The City

Forts erected by the French, mostly during periods of Native American unrest, gave permanence to east-central Wisconsin's most populous community, Green Bay.

The fur trade made up the bedrock of the city's fortunes early on, but Green Bay began growing in earnest upon completion of the Erie Canal in 1825, when the state's first European immigrants descended en masse into Wisconsin, most via Green Bay. Many put down roots immediately, working in Green Bay's burgeoning agricultural, logging, and iron smelting industries; the paper and lumber industry quickly surpassed the beaver trade.

Enormous amounts of ship and railroad transportation still muscle through this to-the-core blue-collar town of tight working-class bungalows.

But remember: History and subtle gentrification notwithstanding, if there is one dominant cultural ethos underpinning the city, it is the *beloved* Green Bay Packers. *The Sporting News*—among many, many other national media—has rated the entire city the number-one sports fans in the National Football League, literally in a league of their own. Need more proof? The waiting list for season tickets is longer than a phone book in a midsize city; at present if you apply now, you'll get tickets in about 200 years. This is a city where 60,000 people pay to watch a *practice*.

Orientation

Cupping Green Bay and bisected by the Fox River, streets can sometimes be a confusing jumble. Always keep in mind which side of the river you're on, and when in doubt, head for Lake Michigan and start over.

(THE PACK

One of the oldest professional football teams in the United States—and the only community-owned team in professional sports—the Green Bay Packers are *it* in this town; check out the glazed-eyed, slobbering Packer fans from around the globe jumping in glee in renovated-but-still-classic Lambeau Field's parking lot. Perhaps no stadium mixes tradition with modernity more than this national treasure. Fans care only that they can visit the stadium virtually every single day of the year! The atrium and its restaurants and shops are open 8 A.M.–9 P.M. daily except game days (till midnight Friday and Saturday); you'd be surprised how many people are wandering around at 8:30 A.M.

Tourists and locals often crowd the free, twice-a-day practices (usually 8:15 A.M. and 2:30 P.M.-ish) during the Packers' late-summer **training camp,** held at the practice facility along Oneida Street across from Lambeau Field. Sometimes practices are held indoors in the team's state-of-the-art Hutson Practice Facility. Practices begin in mid-July and run until preseason games begin in late August. There are usually morning practices and less strenuous post-lunch workouts. In mid-July too is the **Packer Hall of Fame Induction Ceremony,** a very big deal to Packers fans.

GREEN BAY

To Marinette and the U.P.

NEW ZOO ★

Green

Bay

To Shawano and Wausau

To Oneida Nation Museum

BAY BEACH AMUSEMENT PARK/ WILDLIFE SANCTUARY

EAST SHORE DR

UW-GREEN BAY

To Door County

TITLETOWN BREWING COMPANY

KAVARNA

FUZZY'S 63

BAY MOTEL & FAMILY RESTAURANT

HOTEL SIERRA

BUS DEPOT

JAKE'S

NEVILLE PUBLIC MUSEUM

MILITARY AVE

CITY STADIUM

CANDLEWOOD SUITES

LAMBEAU FIELD/ GREEN BAY PACKERS HALL OF FAME

THE PACK

CVB

SKIP A STONE DINER

TUNDRA LODGE RESORT AND WATERPARK

KROLL'S

EVE'S SUPPER CLUB

SKY-LIT MOTEL

THE WELLINGTON

NATIONAL RAILROAD MUSEUM

HERITAGE HILL LIVING HISTORY MUSEUM

ALOFT

AUSTIN STRAUBEL INTERNATIONAL AIRPORT

UNION HOTEL

ZIGGEY'S INN

JAMES ST. INN

To Fox Cities

0   2 mi

0   2 km

To Manitowoc and Milwaukee

© AVALON TRAVEL

(You can also catch a glimpse of initial mini-camps, which open as early as April.)

A perfect Packer Country day would go as follows. Start by watching some of the practice sessions; those standing along the fence line to watch are known as "railbirds," and it's a tradition for Packer players to ride local kids' bikes to and from the playing field. Offer your handkerchief to a weeping Packer fan who's come from afar to realize this dream.

You *can't* miss the **Lambeau Field** tour. Visitors explore virtually every corner of this local landmark (except—sadly—the Packers' locker room), including the pressbox, the

visitors' locker room, the skyboxes, and even the field itself. Hour-long tours are given 10 (or 11) A.M.–4 P.M. daily on nongame days; cost is $11 adults.

The number-one Packer destination is the Lambeau Field Atrium, home to the **Green Bay Packers Hall of Fame** (9 A.M.–6 P.M. daily, hours vary for home games, $10 adults). Packers, Packers, Packers. That's all that's here. It's an orgy of fandom. Most fans weep at the life-size re-creation of the 1967 Ice Bowl—the defining moment in making the team the real "America's Team;" kids will have to push adults out of the way to go wild in the interactive zone!

Lambeau Field

Here's the essential stuff for up-to-date information: 888/442-7225 or packers.com!

Other Packer Sights

True fans will also head to **Fuzzy's 63** (2511 W. Mason St., 920/494-6633, www.fuzzys63.com), a bar owned by retired Pack legend Fuzzy Thurston.

The most unusual sight? How about **Skip a Stone Diner** (2052 Holmgren Way, 920/494-9882) in Ashwaubenon. It preserved the stool sat in regularly by a Packer linebacker, the ferocious Ray Nitschke. (The street name Holmgren Way, incidentally, comes from a Packer coach.)

In 2002, a plaza was dedicated at **City Stadium** (1415 E. Walnut St., behind Green Bay East High School), where the Packers played 1925–1956.

Believe it or not, in Packer-nuts (and utterly anti-Chicago *anything*) Green Bay there exists a *Chicago Bears bar!* The **Lorelei Inn** (1412 S. Webster St., 920/432-5921) was originally owned by a Bears fan (and the decor tells it), but his kids are Packers fans! You can expect

good-natured ribbing. It's closed Sundays except when the Pack and Bears clash.

For all things Packers, here are some good websites: packersnews.com, packerforum.com (a global fan site), southendzone.com, packers-bars.com (find a Packer bar wherever you are), oldbagofdonuts.com (Packers fans will fill you in on the name), jsonline.com (Milwaukee's newspaper is kicks for Packers coverage), packers.scout.com (for real football draft geeks), and greenbaypressgazette.com.

During training camp and on select game days, a cheery way to take in the Pack is aboard the **Legends of Lombardi Tour** on a red double-decker bus imported from England. It leaves from the Convention and Visitors Bureau (1901 S. Oneida St., across the street from Lambeau Field, 920/494-9507 or 888/867-3342, www.greenbay.com).

OTHER SIGHTS
Museums

The staggering **National Railroad Museum** (2285 S. Broadway Ave., 920/437-7623, www.nationalrrmuseum.org, 9 A.M.–5 P.M. Mon.–Sat., 11 A.M.–5 P.M. Sun., $9 adults), with more than 80 railroad cars and locomotives, has a respected collection rivaling any in the nation. Available for close-up inspection is personal fave Big Boy, the world's largest steam locomotive. Of course, train rides are also available, five times daily in summer. Included in the admission is a mile-long jaunt on a narrow-gauge railroad.

Perhaps the most unusual state park in Wisconsin is **Heritage Hill Living History Museum** (2640 S. Webster Ave., 920/448-5150, www.heritagehillgb.org, 10 A.M.–4:30 P.M. Mon.–Sat., noon–4:30 P.M. Sun., Apr.–Oct., $8 adults). More than 25 historic buildings from around Wisconsin have been reconstructed at this 50-acre site. Separated into four distinct thematic areas—Pioneers, Military Life, Small Towns, and Agricultural—the buildings include mock-ups of flimsy original sapling-and-bark dwellings of the Jesuits and some of the oldest extant buildings in Wisconsin. All areas are accessible via wagons.

TITLETOWN

It is ever the same: Sunday morning, 11:59 A.M. The network feed fades to black. Then, as always, a still shot of Him. And, slowly, with the melodrama of sports announcers, the voice-over: "The Man. Vincent T. Lombardi." Or, even more powerfully, "Titletown..." It incites goosebumps, followed by the shakes of unvanquishable dumbbell belief.

THE RELIGION

If there are any awards for professional sports fandom, the Pack and its beloved legions sweep – hands down. One grizzled sportswriter wrote, "The Dallas Cowboys were only another football team; the Packers were a practicing religion." If he only knew the ambivalence, the bittersweet...well, *curse* of being born a Packerbacker. (This author was unlucky enough to be born on the demise of the last Packer empire, after Super Bowl II, back in 1968, and don't think his family hasn't reminded him of the lethal coincidence.)

The Green Bay Packers are the only passively proselytizing franchise in all of professional sports. Hard-core travelers and football aficionados will find Packer bars and Packer fan clubs in every state in the union – as far away as jolly old England. I've even found scads of Packer faithful bellowing for Sunday satellite-dish equity as far away as Taiwan and Thailand.

EARLY YEARS

The Packers were founded in 1919 as one of the handful of teams that would eventually make up the National Football League. The team was born in the back room of the *Green Bay Press-Gazette,* where the cigar-chomping sports editor, George Calhoun, and legendary ex-Notre Damer Curly Lambeau agreed to found a local team. They convinced a local industry bigwig to supply a practice field and uniforms, thus obligating the team to call itself the Indian Packing Company Footballers. This was later shortened to you-know-what. Going 10-1 its first season, the dynasty had begun.

After literally passing the hat in the crowd for the first season, the Packers, in need of financial stability, hit upon one of the most unusual money angles in sports. The community issued $5 nondividend public shares in the team; almost beyond logic, the citizens scooped up the stocks.

The *only* nonprofit, community-owned team in professional sports, the Green Bay Packers have become a true anomaly: a small-market team with few fiscal constraints on finding and wooing talent. And they can never desert the town – if they try to move, the organization is dissolved and all money goes for a Veterans of Foreign Wars memorial.

TITLETOWN'S TITLES

After the Packers whomped their opponents in the first season, they became the first NFL team to win three consecutive NFL titles, and they did it twice – 1929-1931 and 1965-1967. In all, they won 11 championships through 1968 and the Lombardi years. In fact, though the Lombardi-led teams get all the glory, the teams of the early years were even more dominant, amassing a 34-5-2 record.

Then the well went dry. Before the 1990s brought in more forceful management, the Packers suffered through their longest drought ever between NFC Central Division Championships: 24 years. Twenty-four long, unbearable, embarrassing years. Still, the fans dutifully packed the stadium every Sunday. They always believed.

But after all those doormat decades, the Packers finally won the Super Bowl again in 1997, which began an always-in-the-playoffs run culminating in yet another notch in the Titletown belt on February 6, 2011, when the Packers defeated the Super Bowl-seasoned Pittsburgh Steelers 31-25 for their record 13th NFL championship and fourth Super Bowl title. The headline in the *Milwaukee Journal-Sentinel* said it all: "Titletown Again." (Although the most apt quote oft-heard after the game was, "The Lombardi trophy is coming home!")

The **Neville Public Museum** (210 Museum Pl., 920/448-4460, www.nevillepublicmuseum.org, 9 A.M.–4 P.M. Mon.–Tues. and Fri.–Sat., 9 A.M.–8 P.M. Wed.–Thurs., noon–5 P.M. Sun., $4 adults) contains art, history, and science exhibits. The outstanding main hall exhibit "On the Edge of the Inland Sea," a 7,500-square-foot diorama of a retreating glacier, is worth admission, as is the impressive view of the city skyline.

Bay Beach Amusement Park

One of my favorites in Green Bay is the anachronistic gathering of more than a dozen rides along the bay shoreline at the Bay Beach Amusement Park (1313 Bay Beach Rd., 920/391-3671, 10 A.M.–9 P.M. daily June–Aug., Sat.–Sun. May and Sept.). The best part: Rides cost as little as *$0.25.*

Bay Beach Wildlife Sanctuary

Up the road from the amusement park is the excellent Bay Beach Wildlife Sanctuary (1660 E. Shore Dr., 920/391-3671, www.baybeachwildlife.com, 8 A.M.–7:30 P.M. daily Apr.–Sept., shorter hours the rest of the year, free), a 700-acre spread with exhibits on Wisconsin fauna, including the very popular timber wolf house.

NEW Zoo

The well-regarded NEW Zoo (4378 Reforestation Rd., 920/448-4466, 9 A.M.–6 P.M. daily Apr.–Oct., less often the rest of the year, $4 adults, free Wed.), eight miles north of Green Bay, allows the animals greater freedom to roam. Animal compounds include Prairie Grassland, Wisconsin Native, and International—you're as likely to see a Galápagos tortoise as you are a Wisconsin red fox. The zoo has tripled in size in recent years and added many new exhibits, including a black-footed penguin zone. A children's area allows interactive experiences.

Side Trip

West of Ashwaubenon is zany **Seymour,** which bills itself as the "Home of the Hamburger,"

purportedly invented here. The townsfolk fete their title with the annual **Burger Fest** the first Saturday in August; they pretty much try to fry a world-record burger (some three tons!) annually. Just check out the enormous burger and Hamburger Charlie on Depot Street, west of WI 55.

ENTERTAINMENT AND EVENTS

For local entertainment listings, check the schedules in the *Green Bay Press-Gazette.*

The Arts

On the University of Wisconsin-Green Bay campus, the smashingly modern **Weidner Center for the Performing Arts** (920/465-2217, www.weidnercenter.com) showcases national and regional musicians, plays, musicals, dance performances, and the annual Green Bay jazz fest. The city boasts its own symphony orchestra and two community theater groups.

Events

Green Bay's hootenanny, **Bayfest** (www.artseventsinc.com), takes place at the UW-Green Bay campus at the beginning of June. The festival includes five musical stages, some 25 international cuisine tents, games, a carnival, and a huge fireworks display.

There's *always* something Packer-oriented going on in late summer as the city gears up for the NFL season.

RECREATION
Trails

The **Fox River Trail** is a 14-mile multipurpose trail stretching along the Fox Valley corridor to Greenleaf. The city is also the departure point for the **Mountain Bay Trail,** an eight-miler linking to trails west to Wausau.

Camping

The camping nearest to Green Bay is toward Door County north on WI 57, 15 miles out of town: **Bay Shore County Park** (920/448-4466, May–Oct.).

Spectator Sports

It's virtually impossible to get *face price* tickets to regular-season Packers games, especially if the Pack's success continues; preseason games are another matter. Call 920/496-5700 for ticket information.

ACCOMMODATIONS

A caveat: Don't even think of showing up in Green Bay on a weekend when the Packers are playing at home with any hope of getting budget lodging, or any lodging for that matter. Try the visitors bureau's website (www.greenbay.com) for links and deals or even the local lodging association's (www.greenbay-getaways.com).

Downtown

It's been surprisingly possible to scare up a $75 room (though most are more) at the extended-stay **Candlewood Suites** (1125 E. Mason St., 920/430-7040, $60–189), which has a phenomenal number of amenities.

Brand-new upmarket digs are right nearby at the much-raved about **Hotel Sierra** (333 Main St., 920/432-4555, www.hotel-sierra.com, $139–179). It's more or less a self-contained city, so everything you need is here, including a free breakfast in the morning.

Southwest: Airport and Stadium

At the **Sky-Lit Motel** (2120 S. Ashland Ave., 920/494-5641, www.skylitmotel.net, $50–85) you get what you pay for, though it's fine for a cheap sleep.

Where Lombardi Avenue swings around to hook up with Military Avenue to the west is the step-up (and this author's home away from home) **Bay Motel** (1301 S. Military Ave., 920/494-3441, $45–75), where all rooms have free movies; some have mini refrigerators.

A boutique hotel for chic youngsters in Packerville? Yup, **Aloft** (465 Pilgrim Way, 920/884-0800, www.aloftgreenbay.com, $95) is a new boutique hotel that is contrapuntal to blue-collar. It's zen chic and very friendly.

Have a family? The only place to head is the **Tundra Lodge Resort and Waterpark** (Lombardi Ave. and Ashland Ave., 920/405-8700, www.tundralodge.com, $129–399), just a hop, skip, and jump from Lambeau Field. Indoor/outdoor waterparks let the kids work up a sweat; then let 'em gorge in the buffet-style restaurant.

De Pere

De Pere has a couple of interesting lodging choices. A new boutique hotel overlooking the Fox River, the **James St. Inn** (201 James St., 920/337-0111, www.jamesstreetinn.com, $74–220) is in a historic mill. Andrew's Restaurant on-site here is fabulous, especially for fish.

FOOD

Don't forget that De Pere also has some fine eateries, especially the ever since-1918 **Union Hotel** (200 N. Broadway, 920/336-6131, $15–30), the most absolutely anachronistic environment (in a good way) you can find in the state.

Vegetarian

No, it's not oxymoronic to be a vegan in Green Bay; it just seems that way. **Kavarna** (143 N. Broadway, 920/430-3200, breakfast and lunch daily, brunch Sat.–Sun., $5–10) is more of a coffee shop with a café complex, but the yam fries (baked!) are worth a trip.

Heartland Fare

If you really want to rub elbows with the locals, check out **⟨ Kroll's,** the best family restaurant in town, with two locations. The more convenient one is on Main Street (1658 Main St., 920/468-4422, 10:30 A.M.–11 P.M. daily, until midnight weekends, $4–11). The other (S. Ridge Road, closer to Lambeau Field, 920/497-1111) is the older of the two and appears to have come straight out of the movie *Diner.* They serve great walleye and perch along with legendary burgers. This Kroll's also features wall buzzers that customers can use to summon the wait staff.

Kroll's competition is **Bay Family Restaurant** (Military Ave. and 9th St.,

EAST-CENTRAL WATERS

920/494-3441, breakfast, lunch, and dinner daily, $6–11). The Bay uses ingredients direct from family farms and serves homemade pies and piles of hash browns the size of encyclopedias. There are two other locations: 1245 East Mason Street and 1100 Radisson Street. All are open for three squares per day.

Supper Clubs and Fine Dining

Green Bay has every right to argue that it does the supper club as well as Milwaukee in numbers and quality. For exquisite rib-eye steak, **Ziggey's Inn** (741 Hoffman Rd., 920/339-7820, 5–9 P.M. Tues.–Sun., $7–18) can't be beat. Even better is the time-warp aspect of the place—you can imagine Packer teams of the 1960s sitting around digging in.

The Wellington (1060 Hansen Rd., 920/499-2000, lunch and dinner Mon.–Fri., dinner Sat., $8–28) is a Green Bay institution of sorts. An exclusive spot done up as an English drawing room, it specializes in beef Wellington (no surprise) and excellent duck, steer tenderloin, and seafood dishes.

Eve's Supper Club (2020 Riverside Dr., 920/435-1571, lunch and dinner Mon.–Fri., dinner Sat., $12–50) has the grandest view of any dining establishment, perched atop the 2020 Riverside office building overlooking the Fox River, almost directly across from the railroad museum. You most certainly pay for your view.

Brewpubs

Green Bay's got a couple of lively brewpubs. Right downtown at the west end of the Fox River Bridge along WI 29 is **Titletown Brewing Company** (200 Dousman St., 920/437-2337, 11 A.M.–11 P.M. daily, $8–15), with an above-average menu of quite creative fare. It's housed in a grand old depot with a soaring clock tower—great environs! To be fair, virtually across the street, the **Hinterland** (920/438-8050, dinner daily, $8–18) has great beer and phenomenal, way-above-pub-grub food—even caribou, wild boar and the like. The food is not just for kicks; it's professionally well made.

Italian and Pizza

Italian restaurants are the dominant ethnic specialty in Green Bay. One of the best-known is **Victoria's** (2610 Bay Settlement Rd., 920/468-8070, lunch Mon.–Sat., dinner daily, $5–15). Let's not quibble over that stupid word "authenticity"—the portions are outrageously huge; vegetarians also have good options.

The best pizza in town is at **Jake's** (1149 Main St., 920/432-8012, 4 P.M.–midnight Mon.–Sat., 2 P.M.–midnight Sun., $4–6). You'll have to wait up to half an hour for a seat at times, but it, too, is well worth the time.

INFORMATION

The Packer Country Tourism Office (1901 S. Oneida St., 920/494-9507 or 888/867-3342, www.greenbay.com) is across the street from Lambeau Field. It actually serves Green Bay east to Two Rivers, Kewaunee, and Algoma.

The *Green Bay Press-Gazette* is Wisconsin's oldest newspaper, started in 1833 as the *Green Bay Intelligencer;* it's a great source of local goings-on.

GETTING THERE
By Air

Austin Straubel International Airport (920/498-4800), in southwest Green Bay off WI 172, is served by six airlines and more than 50 flights daily to Milwaukee, Chicago, Cleveland, Denver, Detroit, Milwaukee, and Minneapolis.

By Bus

The **bus depot** (800 Cedar St., 920/432-4883) is served by Greyhound (and two on-off regional lines) to most points in southern and western Wisconsin and west to Minnesota.

GETTING AROUND
Organized Tours

The *Foxy Lady* (920/432-3699, Tues.–Sun. mid-Apr.–mid-Oct.), docked behind the Holiday Inn City Centre, offers sightseeing, lunch, cocktail, sunset, dinner, and moonlight cruises. Rates start at $15 for a narrated cruise and go up to $38 for a sunset dinner.

Reservations are required for all but the sightseeing cruise.

ONEIDA NATION

West of Green Bay are the 12 square miles making up the **Oneida Indian Reservation.** Known as the "People of the Standing Stone," the Oneida were members of the League of the Iroquois and once a protectorate of the Stockbridge-Munsee bands on the east coast. They moved westward en masse (save for a small band still in New York) not long after the turn of the 18th century.

One of the only repositories of the history of the Oneida is the **Oneida Nation Museum** (W892 EE Rd., 920/869-2768, 9 A.M.–5 P.M. Tues.–Fri., 10 A.M.–5 P.M. Sat., $2 adults, $1 children). Exhibits in the main hall focus on Oneida history and culture; a longhouse and stockade are outside, as well as a nice nature trail. The Oneida **powwow** takes place on or near the Fourth of July.

The Bottom of the Door

For many folks, Door County begins only when they have buzzed the bridge spanning Sturgeon Bay's Lake Michigan canal; others claim that you're not in the county until WI 42 and WI 57 bifurcate into bayside and lakeside routes northeast of town. Still, Door County proper includes a chunk of 15 or more miles south of the ship channel, and the *peninsula* comprises underappreciated Kewaunee County, east of Green Bay, as well.

Note that WI 57 has been undergoing dramatic changes and this will likely continue as long as tourists flock to the Door. The road bends away from the lake and into a hyperdrive four-lane divided highway. And up the peninsula this may creep. (Somehow transportation engineers have to figure out a way to plat the road and not damage archaeological sites, wetlands, and threatened species, all of which have slowed the project.) For now, along WI 57, you'll find an easy-to-overlook little county wayside. At **Red Banks** wayside, a statue to Jean Nicolet stands a few hundred yards from the red clay bluffs overlooking the serene bay. Those in the know agree that it was here that Jean Nicolet first came sloshing ashore in 1634, cracking his harquebuses to impress the Winnebago.

But WI 57 leaves much to the imagination. More adventuresome travelers might attempt to find Highway A out of Green Bay; it spins along the same route, but right atop the lake. Bypassing Point Sable—once a boundary between Native American tribal lands—the road offers views of a state wildlife area across the waters. Farther up, you can see Vincent Point and, immediately after that, Red Banks itself. This byway continues through Benderville before linking with WI 57 again (there's camping in a county park up the road) before crossing the Kewaunee-Door County line into Belgian territory.

BRUSSELS AND VICINITY

Brussels and surrounding towns such as Champion, Euren, Maplewood, Rosiere, and Forestville constitute the country's largest Belgian-American settlement. The architecture of the region is so well preserved that more than 100 buildings make up Wisconsin's first *rural* National Historical Landmark. Right along WI 57, the homes and Catholic chapels show distinctive Belgian influences along with a lot of reddish-orange brick and split cedar fencing. On alternating weekends through the summer, the villages still celebrate *Kermiss,* church Mass during harvest season.

Brussels is the area's capital of sorts, with **Belgian Days** the first week of July—plenty of Belgian chicken, *booyah* (thick vegetable stock), *jute* (boiled cabbage), and tripe sausage. You'll find Belgian fare in a few places in Brussels, including **Marchants Food, Inc.** (9674 WI 57, 920/825-1244, 8 A.M.–8 P.M. Mon.–Fri., 8 A.M.–6 P.M. Sat., 8 A.M.–12:30 P.M. Sun.), open daily for 50 years.

A quick side trip takes in lots of Belgian architecture. In Robinsville, a mile and a half east of Champion along Highway K, sits the **shrine grotto,** a home and school for disabled children founded by a Belgian to whom the Virgin Mary is said to have appeared in 1858.

Not Belgian per se but north of Luxemburg, itself south of Brussels, near the junction of Highways A and C is **Joe Rouer's** (920/866-2585), a classic bar with legendary burgers that this author would love to eat right now. The cheese curds are pretty darned good, as well.

North of Brussels along Highway C, the **St. Francis Xavier Church and Grotto Cemetery** is representative of Belgian rural construction; farmers contributed aesthetically pleasing stones from their fields to raise a grotto and crypt for the local reverend.

Three miles northeast of Brussels via Highway C is the **Gardner Swamp State Wildlife Area** along Keyes Creek.

KEWAUNEE

Perched on a hillside overlooking a lovely historic harbor, Kewaunee was once bent on rivaling Chicago as maritime center of the Great Lakes and could likely have given the Windy City a run for its money when an influx of immigrants descended after hearing rumors of a gold strike in the area. But Chicago had the rail, while Kewaunee, despite its harbor, was isolated and became a minor port and lumber town.

Sights

Kewaunee is Wisconsin's Czech nerve center. Outlying villages show a Czech/Bohemian heritage and you'll often hear Czech spoken. Five miles south of town via WI 42 is

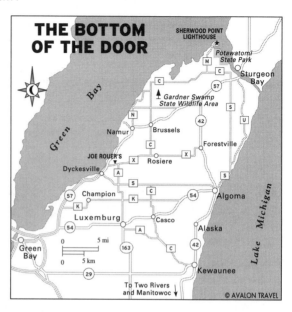

a new **Heritage Farm** (920/388-0604), an 1876 Czech homestead renovated into a sort of cultural center; open by appointment or during events (of which there seems always to be one).

The chamber of commerce has maps of a nifty **walking tour,** taking in about three dozen historical structures. Everybody snaps a shot of the 1909 **Kewaunee pierhead lighthouse.** The structure consists today of a steel frame base and steel tower with a cast-iron octagonal lantern about 50 feet high. At the harbor you can take a tour ($3) aboard a retired World War II **tugboat.** The central **Old Jail Museum** (Vlier and Dodge, 920/388-4410, noon–4 P.M. daily in summer, free) is near the courthouse in an old sheriff's home, part of which doubled as the jail, with gruesome dungeon cells. Statues of Father Marquette and solemn, pious Potawatomi are likely what you'll be shown first. Head, too, for the replica of the USS *Pueblo.* The ill-fated Navy ship, involved in an incident with North Korea in the 1950s, was built in Kewaunee during World War II.

Three miles west of town, the Wisconsin Department of Natural Resources operates a state-of-the-art **Anadromous Fish Facility** (N3884 Ransom Moore Ln., 920/388-1025, 10 A.M.–5 P.M. daily, free). Detailed are the spawning practices of anadromous fish, viewed through underwater panels.

Southwest of town in Montpelier township is a **Rustic Road** scenic drive involving parts of Hrabik, Cherneysville, Sleepy Hollow, and Pine Grove Roads. Close to here, south of Krok, is the only known Wisconsin rooftop windmill, a granddaddy of a historic structure.

At **Svoboda Industries** along WI 42 North, you'll see what is purportedly the world's largest grandfather clock—39 feet tall.

The local visitors information center (920/388-4822 or 800/666-8214, www.kewaunee.org) is right on WI 42, north of downtown, near a great marsh walk.

Accommodations

On the harbor is the **Harrison Harbour House** (920/388-0606, $35!), built for a former governor and best described by the proprietors as a "hunting cabin for fishermen," with bunk beds, stone walls, rough-hewn board ceilings, and a definite feel of lake life. It isn't for everyone, but some folks just groove on it.

The **Historic Karsten Inn** (122 Ellis St., 920/388-3800, www.karsteninn.com, from $90) is a B&B rebuilt from a real inn; they've also got a bistro-esque dining room.

If Door County camping is too far away, $15 gets you a basic site at **Kewaunee Village** (333 Terraqua Dr., 800/274-9684), north of town along WI 42; a nature area has trails.

Food

The local specialty is Czechoslovakian and Bohemian food, including *kolace* (yeast buns with fruit filling) and *buhuite* (pronounced bu-ta—thin dough filled with seeds or fruit), sauerkraut rye bread, and *rohlik*. These delectable baked goods are available at **Tom's Pastry Shop** (409 WI 42, 920/388-2533), which is also a deli. Near the bridge in town are a couple of places for great smoked fish.

ALGOMA

The whole drive along WI 42 from Manitowoc to Algoma is spectacular—a resplendent, beach-hugging route. As you swoop into Algoma from the south, seemingly endless miles of wide, empty beach begin, both road and beach unencumbered by travelers. This freshly scrubbed little community of friendly folks might be said to be a wonderful poor man's Door County (were one to approve of such distinctions).

The small town is known today mostly for its killer sportfishing, and its marinas account for the state's most substantial sportfishing industry with four—count 'em—state records.

At the time of writing, a new passenger ferry between Algoma to Frankfort, MI, was being bandied about; once a pipe dream, it's actually gaining traction as of late.

Sights

Von Stiehl Winery (115 Navarino St., 920/487-5208, www.vonstiehl.com, guided tours 9:30 A.M.–4:30 P.M. daily May–Oct., 2 P.M. Sat. rest of year, $3.75 adults) is the oldest licensed winery in Wisconsin, housed in what was once the Ahnapee Brewery (named after the local river), built in the 1850s, whose three-foot-thick limestone walls are a ready-made underground catacomb system. The house specialty is cherry wine; many other Wisconsin fruit wines are produced, all guarded by a patented system to prevent premature aging and light damage.

Algoma is also the southern terminus of the **Ahnapee State Trail,** a section of the Ice Age National Scenic Trail stretching 18 miles partially along the Ahnapee River to the southern fringe of Sturgeon Bay. Another trail runs from Algoma to Casco.

Algoma once had a legendary "fishing mayor," Art Dettman. His name lives on in a restored fish shanty—a quasi-museum to fishing—on the National Register of Historic Places. It's open by appointment only; call 920/487-3443 for information.

Algoma has, without a doubt, the cutest

movie theater in Wisconsin—my living room is larger.

Charter Fishing

Second in the state for fish taken, this is a prime place to smear on the zinc oxide and do the Ahab thang. Early-season lake trout are generally hot in May, but June is Algoma's biggest month; rainbow trout and chinook salmon are everywhere. Steelhead and especially king salmon are added to the mix come July, and brown trout get big in August. September fishing is great.

Camping

Ahnapee River Trails Campground (E6053 W. Wilson Rd., 920/487-5777, $18) is on the Ahnapee River Trail.

Accommodations

A basic motel that may not be right atop Lake Michigan (it's all of across the road), the **Algoma Beach Motel** (2221 Lake St., 920/487-3214, $79) has clean rooms and a very welcoming owner.

Food

Several family restaurants and diners in town serve Belgian *booyah* and Belgian pie. For espresso, coffee, tea, or light food—along with live music—in a trendy atmosphere, you can't beat **Caffe Tlazo** (607 WI 42, 920/487-7240, 6 A.M.–8 P.M. Mon.–Fri., 7 A.M.–8 P.M. Sat., 7 A.M.–7 P.M. Sun., $5 and up). Casual dining is at the historic **Hotel Stebbins** (201 Steele St., 920/487-5526, www.thehotelstebbins. com, 4:30–10 P.M. daily during peak season, 5–9 P.M. Tues.–Sat. rest of year, $8–25), where they often have live music.

For a picnic basket, **Bearcat's** (WI 42 and Navarino St., 920/487-2372, 9 A.M.–5 P.M. daily year-round) has great smoked fish for dirt cheap prices!

Information and Services

The tourist information center (920/487-2041 or 800/498-4888, www.algoma.org) is on the south edge of Algoma along WI 42. It is also the departure point for historical walking tours of downtown—on your own or guided ($3).

Appleton

I've seen it referred to as the Queen of the Fox Cities and the Princess of Paper Valley (though one local thought a bit and pointed out that if you said that here, no one would know what city you were talking about!). Bisected by the Fox River, this spread-out city hardly seems paper-centered industrial when you're traipsing about the gentrified downtown area.

One civic nucleus is well-respected Lawrence University, a small liberal-arts college that was the state's first co-ed institution of higher education and also the first to initiate a postgraduate papermaking institute.

Appleton grew up around a mill, but wheat production was far more profitable than floating log rafts. Not until after the Civil War did local industrialists turn their attention to Wisconsin's ready-made paper wealth. It is still so—the region is known alternatively as Paper Valley.

The Fox Cities and Fox Valley

Between Neenah and Kaukauna along Lake Winnebago's northwestern cap lie a dozen concatenate communities making up the Fox Cities region—a region part of but distinct from the Fox River Valley, which itself stretches along the Fox River–Lake Winnebago corridor and takes in all communities between Green Bay and Oshkosh. Appleton is the region's economic anchor; the smallest town is Combined Locks. All take their inspiration from the Fox River—one of the few rivers in North America to flow north. Together, the Fox Cities constitute the third-largest metropolitan area in the state (pop. 180,000), a statistic many Wisconsinites find surprising.

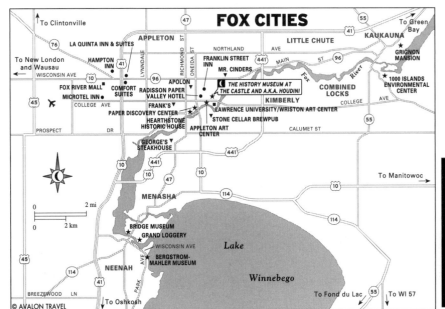

SIGHTS

◖ The History Museum at the Castle and A.K.A. Houdini

Paper may be the raison d'etre, but folks just can't get enough of that Houdini magic. Born Ehrich Weiss in Hungary in 1874, the enigmatic Houdini spent most of his life in Appleton. A.K.A. Houdini (330 E. College Ave., 920/735-8445, www.myhistorymuseum.org) is maintained as part of The History Museum at the Castle. The foremost collection of Houdini artifacts anywhere includes the Guiteau handcuffs, which bound President Garfield's assassin and from which the magician later escaped. The center has prepared a detailed walking tour of the city (marked with brass plaques), taking in the sites of his childhood. Magic shows, hands-on exhibits, and more thrill kids (and parents).

The museum (330 E. College Ave., 920/735-9370) itself contains an excellent and award-winning exhibit ("Tools of Change") on the workers and economic history of the Lower Fox region.

The museums are open 10 A.M.–4 P.M. Tuesday–Saturday, till 8 P.M. Thurs., noon–4 P.M. Sunday June–August, closed Monday the rest of the year. Admission is $7.50.

Paper Discovery Center

Where else should the Paper Industry Hall of Fame (425 W. Water St., 920/749-3040, www.paperdiscoverycenter.org, 10 A.M.–4 P.M. Mon.–Sat., $5) go but the Fox River Valley, of which Appleton is the queen? In a renovated paper mill, experience every facet of paper, start to finish—with lots of activities for the kids.

Hearthstone Historic House

Hearthstone Historic House (625 W. Prospect Ave., 920/730-8204, 10 A.M.–3:30 P.M Tues–Fri., 11 A.M.–3:30 P.M. Sat., 1–3:30 P.M. Sun., $6 adults) is a massive 1882 Victorian. Within Appleton's city limits, the old Fox drops almost 40 feet, much of it in angry rapids. In the late 1880s the Hearthstone, the city's major

JOSEPH MCCARTHY

I have in my hands a list of 205 names that were made known to the Secretary of State as being members of the Communist Party and who nevertheless are still working and shaping policy in the State Department.

Uttered by Senator Joseph McCarthy (a Fox Cities native) in Wheeling, West Virginia, these words – in what became known as the 205 Speech – thrust him into the national political spotlight. Before he shot himself in the foot politically, he dominated U.S. politics, electrified the nation, aided Tricky Dick, and inspired a new word. Wisconsinites still wonder how they feel about one of their most infamous native sons. (And after passage of the post-9/11 Patriot Act, his name was being brought up again and again.)

TAIL GUNNER JOE

After a lifelong struggle with education, McCarthy graduated from Marquette Law and astonished everyone by winning a judgeship in 1938 through sheer grassroots, flesh-pressing toil.

He was not, shall we say, a widely respected judge. He further infuriated opponents by stumping for higher office – by exaggerating, some say – from the South Pacific, while in World War II; Tail Gunner Joe was born.

THE JUNIOR SENATOR

McCarthy was swept up in the GOP wave of 1946 and made it to Washington, besting La Follette (the name is legendary here). He incessantly angered the Senate with his in-tractable attitude, personal attacks, and rules violations. By 1949, the congressional leadership loathed him, and most assumed he was simply a lame-duck embarrassment.

What no one counted on was his shrewd prescience about the national paranoia over Communism. In part, McCarthy concocted the Red Scare. He was once again reelected. His path culminated in his antics in the Special House Committee on Un-American Activities. McCarthyism was born.

By 1953, he had reached the pinnacle of his powers, attacking his peers and fending off censure attempts from his many Senate enemies. One charge finally stuck – a kickback scheme. On December 2, 1954, he was officially censured, diminishing the blindly firing junior senator from Wisconsin.

WISCONSIN AND MCCARTHY

Was he a nutcase obscenity? A prescient, passionate Red fighter? Strident opposition to McCarthy was everpresent throughout his reign. The large press in Madison and Milwaukee lobbed as many editorial shells as it could to bring him down. "Joe Must Go" recall petitions collected with almost half a million signatures statewide.

Ask Wisconsinites today about McCarthy and they'll likely dodge the question or roll their eyes and shudder. There *are* still those who support him.

Perhaps most tellingly, Appleton, his adopted hometown, removed his bust (and all other signs) from the courthouse, while favorite resident Harry Houdini is celebrated with Houdini Plaza and its huge memorial sculpture smack in the city center.

---

architectural draw, was the first home to be lighted by a self-contained hydroelectric plant (the United States' first mostly electric streetcar line went up simultaneously). The rich original appointments have been preserved, down to period electroliers and light switches designed by Thomas Edison. Hands-on displays teach visitors about electricity and allow you to operate the controls of a power plant.

Art Galleries

Lawrence University's **Wriston Art Center** (E. College Ave., 920/832-6621, hours vary Tues.–Sat., free) features rotating and permanent exhibits of student and guest artists in traditional and mixed media. If for no other reason, go to see the building's otherworldly design.

The **Appleton Art Center** (130 N. Morrison St., 920/733-4089, www.appletonartcenter.

org, hours vary Mon.–Sat., free) has three galleries, with an emphasis on regional artists, and hosts the largest summer art fair in the state. The Fine Art Exhibition showcases Fox River Valley artists.

Side Trips
In nearby New London, along the Wolf River, the **Mosquito Hill Nature Center** (N3880 Rogers Rd., 920/779-6433) offers some good hiking trails and the very intriguing Wisconsin Butterfly House, showcasing Wisconsin's native butterfly species. The American water spaniel, bred by a local resident, also originated in New London.

Among the oldest paved trails in Wisconsin is hard-to-find number 53 on Wisconsin's Rustic Road system. Beginning in 1857, work was done on what today are Garrity, McCabe, Greiner, and Bodde Roads, northwest of Appleton along U.S. 41 at Highway JJ. (Keep your eyes peeled—it's somewhat confusing.) Along the way, you'll pass scenic double-arch bridges, a stone silo, and a wildlife conservation area.

ENTERTAINMENT AND EVENTS
Pick up a copy of the free monthly *Scene,* which has a good listing of entertainment and cuisine. Also check out appletondowntown.org.

Pubs and Nightspots
Park Central (318 W. College Ave., 920/738-5603) comprises a half dozen bars, comedy clubs, and sports bars. Closer to Lawrence University, one place to check out is **Houdini's Lounge** (117 S. Appleton St., 920/832-8615), a pub with Houdini as a central theme (no surprise) and more than 60 beers available.

Packed to the rafters is **Cleo's Brown Beam** (205 W. College Ave.), which bills itself the "Cheers of Appleton" and has an amazing display of Christmas lights all year. **Bazil's** (109 W. College Ave., 920/954-1770) features an amazing 135 microbrews.

The **Stone Cellar Brewpub** (1004 Olde Oneida St., 920/735-0507) is an 1858 brewery

that whips out a few tasty brands—one named for Houdini.

USA Today called **The Wooden Nickel** (217 E. College Ave., 920/735-0661) the best sports bar in Wisconsin, and it's hard to argue with that.

But yours truly loves **Olde Town Tavern** (107 W. College Ave., 920/954-0103) for its wonderful beers of yesteryear (Schlitz? Really? How grandfatherly!).

Cultural Events
Lawrence University has almost always got something happening, from a remarkable speaker series to regular performing arts productions at the Memorial Chapel and Stansbury Theatre, in the Music-Drama Center. For information, contact the Office of Public Events (920/832-6585).

SHOPPING
Malls
Appleton is mall country, with so much mall space that bus tours make regular pilgrimages here. (The city sported the nation's first indoor mall—though it was demolished partially in 2006 for a new complex.) The unity of the **Fox River Mall** (4301 W. Wisconsin Ave., 920/739-4100), the state's second-largest indoor mall, is admirable (add up the shops surrounding it, and it's the highest concentration in the state!).

SPORTS AND RECREATION
Spectator Sports
Goodland Field (2400 N. Casaloma Dr., 920/733-4152) is the home of the Wisconsin Timber Rattlers, a single-A minor league franchise of the Milwaukee Brewers. It's typical family-friendly fun with zany promotions and dirt-cheap prices!

ACCOMMODATIONS
West of downtown are most lodgings, including the value **Microtel Inn** (321 Metro Dr., 920/997-3121, $52 s or d), with an exercise room and whirlpool. The Appleton **Hampton Inn** (350 Fox River Dr., 920/954-9211, $95) has been rated one of the top 10 Hampton Inns nationwide.

EAST-CENTRAL WATERS

One of the largest recreation centers in the state is at the Appleton **Comfort Suites Comfort Dome** (3809 W. Wisconsin Ave., 920/730-3800, $100). Some rooms have kitchens and microwaves.

A few blocks north of the Avenue Mall is the 1897 Victorian **Franklin Street Inn** (318 E. Franklin St., 920/739-3702, www.franklinstreetinn.com, from $99). Original pocket doors, oak and maple hardwoods, and original chandeliers give the place—one of the stateliest mansions in town—a nice feel.

Trim **La Quinta Inn & Suites** (3730 W. College Ave., 920/734-9231, $99 s or d) was just refurbished and offers two pools, sauna, whirlpool, a dining room, and continental breakfast.

Downtown, newest is the European-style boutique hotel **CopperLeaf Boutique Hotel** (300 W. College Ave., 877/303-0303, www.copperleafhotel.com, from $140), a great deal considering the location, the freshness of the place, and amenities. Folks rave about it.

Just a skip across the street, the **Radisson Paper Valley Hotel** (333 W. College Ave., 920/733-8000, $209) features more than 400 rooms of all types. Take a look at some before checking in.

FOOD

Man, downtown Appleton has just an amazing array of eateries. Just stroll a few blocks and you'll pretty much cover the world!

Pizza

Frank's (815 W. College Ave., 920/734-9131, 4 P.M.–3 A.M. daily, $4–9) has been making every ingredient of its pizzas from scratch for more than 40 years—including the sausage—and it's still going strong. If nothing else, head for the 18-piece brass big band blowouts, held October–May.

Heartland Fare

Popular with Appleton residents is **Mr. Cinders** (1309 E. Wisconsin Ave., 920/738-0100, 10:30 A.M.–late daily, $4–9). You can't go wrong with the burgers or the delicious grilled steak sandwich. Best of all, there's a fish fry all day Friday.

Steaks and Supper Clubs

Open for 50 years and still going strong is **(George's Steak House** (2208 S. Memorial Dr., 920/733-4939, lunch and dinner Mon.–Fri., dinner Sat., $5–20). It's strictly steaks and seafood here, with piano music nightly.

Others point out that this is Packerland, after all, so a visit to **Vince Lombardi's Steakhouse** (333 W. College Ave., 920/380-9390, 4–10 P.M. Mon.–Sat., till 9 P.M. Sun., $15–45) in the Radisson Paper Valley Hotel is a requisite—and in fact the steaks are sublime!

Well, hold on, there is also the coolly upscale **Black and Tan Grille** (300 W. College Ave., 920/380-4745, lunch Mon.–Fri., dinner nightly, $20–32) for contemporary American with great steaks and seafood.

Asian

For an upscale Pacific Rim-Asian fusion meal, head directly to **(Cy's Asian Bistro** (208 W. Wisconsin Ave., 920/969-9549, lunch and dinner Mon.–Fri., dinner Sat., $10–16), whose remarkable food has heavy overtones of Thai. And Cy is one of the friendliest proprietors you'll ever chat with at your table.

Mediterranean

One of the best dining experiences of late has come at **Apolon** (207 N. Appleton St., 920/939-1122, 5–10 P.M. Mon.–Sat., $9–20), a pan-Mediterranean (Hellenic heavy) restaurant, famed for their flaming cheese.

INFORMATION AND SERVICES

The Fox Cities Convention and Visitors Bureau (3433 W. College Ave., 920/734-3358 or 800/236-6673, www.foxcities.org) is actually quite far west of downtown, but the staff is definitely helpful.

GETTING THERE
By Bus

Greyhound (100 E. Washington St., 920/733-

2318) has frequent daily departures to major regional cities. **Lamers** bus line (800/261-6600) also has one departure daily to Milwaukee's Amtrak station and one to Wausau.

By Air
The **Outagamie County Airport** (www. atwairport.com) is the fourth-busiest in Wisconsin (60 flights daily).

Vicinity of Appleton

NEENAH-MENASHA
The twin cities of Neenah-Menasha are casually regarded as one entity, though their governments are separate. They share Doty Island, where Little Lake Butte des Mortes of the Fox River empties into Lake Winnebago.

Two Fox River channels flowing past the island and two minor promontories made available ready-made water power and gave rise to the birth of both villages by the 1840s. Depressed industries spurred papermaking, and within three decades Neenah-Menasha ruled the powerful Wisconsin papermaking region.

Bergstrom-Mahler Museum
This massive dwelling was once home to early area industrialist John Bergstrom. The highlight of the museum (165 N. Park Ave., 920/751-4658, 10 A.M.–4:30 P.M. Tues.–Fri., 9 A.M.–4:30 P.M. Sat., 1–4:30 P.M. Sun., free) is a world-renowned collection of paperweights, many dating from the French classic era of 1845–1860. The glass menagerie, as the museum calls it, is made up of 2,100 exquisite pieces.

Downtown Neenah and Menasha Riverfront
The scenic, landscaped Fox River north channel sports walkways with a kid-friendly fountain and summer concerts; the rest of the twin towns feature a marina and more than 30 picturesque historic buildings, many straight neoclassical in design. The best view is from the still-hand-operated lock on the canal. A new museum along Tayco Street, the **Bridge Tower Museum** (10 A.M.–7 P.M. daily May–Nov., free), is in an 80-year-old bridgetender's tower.

Downtown Neenah's East Wisconsin Avenue gives the best glimpse into 19th-century opulence and great river vistas. The mansions along this stretch were the partial setting for Wisconsin native Edna Ferber's novel *Come and Get It.*

Neenah's Doty Park contains a reconstruction of **Grand Loggery** (noon–4 P.M. daily June–Aug.), the home of James Doty, the state's second territorial governor. Artifacts of family and area history are scant, however.

Menasha's **Smith Park** has a few Native American burial mounds. **Kimberly Point Park,** at the confluence of Lake Winnebago and the Fox River, has a great lighthouse and some good views of the river. The big draw is the world-class **Barlow Planetarium** (1478 Midway Rd., 920/832-2848, fox.uwc.edu, $6 adults for public shows), on the campus of UW-Fox Valley. It has virtual reality exhibits and new public shows every week; no reservations required.

Adjacent to the planetarium is the **Weis Earth Science Museum** (1478 Midway Rd., 920/832-2925, hours vary, $2), the official mineralogical museum of the state. You wanna know what's what about glaciers and the stunning sandstone formations of the state? Right here's the place.

An FYI: in Menasha, the **Club Tavern** (56 Racine St., 920/722-2452) is one of this author's favorite low-key taverns. Lots of off-beat beers on tap and friendly proprietors.

KAUKAUNA
The word *gran ka-ka-lin* is a French-Ojibwa pidgin hybrid describing the long portage once necessary to trek around the city's 50-foot cascades, which ultimately required five locks to

tame. A bit more amusing: In 1793, the area's land was purchased—the first recognized deed in the state—for the princely sum of two barrels of rum.

Sights

Not far from the pesky rapids of old stands **Grignon Mansion** (Augustine St., 920/766-3122, noon–4 P.M. Fri. and Sun., $4 adults). Built in 1838 by Augustin Grignon, to replace the log shack lived in by rum-dealing city founder Dominique Ducharme, the house became known as the mansion in the woods. It has been thoroughly renovated, down to the hand-carved newel posts and imposing brick fireplaces—the apple orchard still stands. (Though from the outside it doesn't look much like a "mansion.") Several of Kaukauna's legendary locks can be reached via the grounds.

Across the river at a bight is the aptly named **1000 Islands Environmental Center** (700 Dodge St., 920/766-4733, 8 A.M.–4 P.M. Mon.–Fri., 10 A.M.–4 P.M. Sat.–Sun., free), a vital stop on the Mississippi Flyway for waterfowl and predatory birds. A huge number of mounted animals are displayed, and live versions include plenty of native Wisconsin fauna, such as great blue heron, coot, and bitterns. The acreage also supports a stand of chinquapin oak, rare in the state. Plenty of great trails run along the Fox River here.

❰ HIGH CLIFF STATE PARK

The vista from this sheer escarpment northeast of Lake Winnebago is truly sublime. The cliff is actually the western edge of the Niagara Escarpment, a jutting, blufflike dolomite rise stretching almost 1,000 miles to the east, through Door County and beyond to Niagara Falls. From the top, almost 250 feet above the waters, you can see all of the Fox River Valley—Appleton, Oshkosh, Neenah, Menasha, and Kaukauna. Perhaps we should do as Chief Redbird of the Ojibwa did; he loved to sit on the cliff and "listen" to the lake—his statue still does today.

High Cliff was founded on an old limestone quarrying and kiln operation. Extant

Grignon Mansion, modest but historically perfect

© THOMAS HUHTI

EAST-CENTRAL WATERS

© THOMAS HUHTI

lime kilns aging gracefully, High Cliff State Park

materiel and former Western Lime and Cement Company structures still stand. Effigy mounds (28–285 feet long) found along trails originated from an unknown prehistoric Native American tribe.

Recreation

Southeast of Appleton approximately 12 miles, the park (920/989-1106, day use 6 A.M.–11 P.M. daily) maintains both a swimming beach and an 85-slip marina. Hikers have seven miles of somewhat steep trails to choose from, and cross-country skiers have access to four of those come winter. The **Lime-Kiln Trail** is just over two miles and runs from the lime kiln ruins to the lake and then up the east side of the escarpment. The longest is the **Red Bird Trail,** mostly gentle and passing by the family campground.

Camping

The park's 1,200 acres have 112 fairly isolated campsites (920/989-1106), most occupied early in the high season.

Oshkosh

Former President Jimmy Carter once said in a speech at the University of Wisconsin-Oshkosh campus, "I have never seen a more beautiful, clean, and attractive place." He was referring to this Fox River Valley city of 55,000—the one with the weird name. Situated on the western bight of Lake Winnebago and bisected by the Fox River, the city is often associated, by both Wisconsinites and outsiders, with two disparate images—bib overalls and bizarre airplanes. Since 1895, Oshkosh B'Gosh has turned out functional, fashionable bib overalls and children's clothing and launched the city's tongue-twisting name onto the international

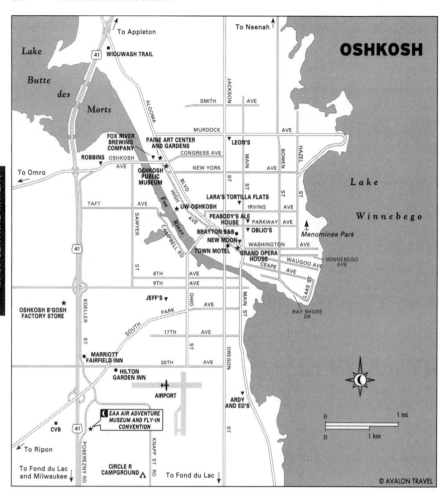

scene. (And, yes, they *have* heard people say things such as "Is this Oshkosh, b'gosh?") As for bizarre airplanes, the annual Experimental Aircraft Association's Fly-In is the largest of its kind, a not-to-be-missed highlight of itinerant edge-dwelling avionics.

History

Strategically located, waterwise, Oshkosh had always been a historic gathering spot for Native Americans. The primary Jesuit Black Robe himself, Father Jean Claude Allouez, even came in 1670 to preach to the Fox and Menominee Indians.

SAWDUST CITY

More than a century and a half ago, the north woods of Wisconsin extended much farther south than today. In 1848, the first large-scale sawmills appeared. By the close of the Civil War, about 35 factories were roaring. The result was constant light showers of wood dust—at times an inch thick on the back streets. Hence, Oshkosh earned the moniker "Sawdust City." Excavations along Oshkosh riverbanks still reveal marbled layers of compacted sawdust.

This sawdust condemned the city to a painful series of conflagrations; an 1875 fire was so bad that the city—built of the cheap local timber—finally rebuilt with stone. Ironically, some of this stone came from Chicago, itself recently devastated by fire and rebuilt mostly with wood from Oshkosh sawmills!

◖ EAA AIR ADVENTURE MUSEUM AND FLY-IN CONVENTION

The state has officially decreed this museum (3000 Poberezny Rd., 920/426-4818, www.airventuremuseum.org, 8:30 A.M.–5 P.M. Mon.–Sat., 10 A.M.–5 P.M. Sun., $12.50 adults) a state treasure, a consequence no doubt of the 800,000 or so visitors who converge on Oshkosh for the annual fly-in sponsored by the Experimental Aircraft

Association (EAA). More than 250 airplanes of every possible type are displayed in the museum—aerobatics, home-built, racers, and more. Five theaters, numerous display galleries, and tons of multimedia exhibits make this well worth the admission; kids (of all ages) absolutely adore the many, many hands-on exhibits in the Kidventure Gallery. (I still can't recover from the g-force machine.) Be there when flights are offered in old-timey planes, complete with the leather hat, goggles, and wind-blown hair. The museum is located off U.S. 41 at the WI 44 exit, next to Wittman Regional Airport. All in all, this is perhaps the best money spent for a family in the region.

EAA International Fly-In Convention

Oshkosh aviation pioneer Steve Wittman designed and built racing planes, one of which is on display at the Smithsonian. He was so impressive he drew the attention of Orville Wright and other airplane aficionados. Soon

EAA Fly-in Convention participants roaring by

EAST-CENTRAL WATERS

after the EAA moved to Oshkosh, a tradition began: the gathering known as the Fly-In, now a legendary, jawdropping display of airplanes that draws hundreds of thousands of people from around the world.

And it's certainly a spectacle. The skies in the last week of July and into August are filled with planes and pilots who'll never shake their appetite for aviation the way it used to be done—strictly by the seat of your pants. Handmade and antique aircraft are the highlights, but lots of contemporary military aircraft are also on show. Thrilling air shows go on nonstop. In all, almost 12,000 aircraft and more than 750,000 people are on hand for this one. Remember to wear good shoes, a hat, and sunscreen, and carry water.

The Fly-In is held the last week of July and/or first week of August and runs 8 A.M.–8 P.M. daily; air shows start at 3 P.M. It doesn't come cheap; for nonmembers, prices are $37 a day adults.

OTHER SIGHTS
Paine Art Center and Gardens
A lumber baron's Tudor revival house, this museum (1410 Algoma Blvd., 920/235-6903, 11 A.M.–4 P.M. Tues.–Sun., $9 adults) displays meticulously appointed rooms showcasing period furnishings and antiques, along with 19th-century French Barbizon and U.S. art. Outside lie acres and acres of gardens; one, modeled after the Dutch Pond Garden at Hampton Court in England, features more than 100 varieties of roses. Legend has it the place is haunted, but the caretakers disavow any knowledge.

Oshkosh Public Museum
In a grand 1907 English-style home, this is one of the best public museums you'll see in a town of Oshkosh's size. Permanent holdings range in subject from local and natural history, china, and pressed glass to Native American ethnology and archaeology. One highlight is an eight-foot-tall Apostles Clock designed and built in the late 1800s by a German immigrant; it's considered one of Wisconsin's

---

THE REPUBLIC OF WINNECONNE

In 1967 the state of Wisconsin issued its annual highway map. Puzzled taverngoers in Winneconne – let's get this out of the way now, it's west of Oshkosh – tried to find their village. Gone, absent, forgotten, ignored.

With tongues nudged a bit into cheek, the village board voted to secede from the state; then it declared war. The new Republic of Winneconne's banner boasted: "We like it – where?" To which the governor, in Madison, said smiling, "By the way, where *is* Winneconne?" The brouhaha continued as the little village that wouldn't be ignored went through machinations of re-creating itself as a sovereign nation; all of this as the nation chuckled along with the resulting media barrage. They've never been overlooked since.

---

most treasured pieces of folk art. The museum (1331 Algoma Blvd., 920/424-4731, 10 A.M.–4:30 P.M. Tues.–Sat., 1–4:30 P.M. Sun.) is still, respectably, free.

Grand Opera House
Try to visit this architectural gem (100 High Ave., 920/424-2355), an 1883 edifice designed after majestic halls in Italy.

Oshkosh B'Gosh
This clothier, established in 1895, put Oshkosh on the map, fashion- and functionwise. Tours of the factory, where the dandy pinstriped bib overalls come together, are sadly no longer offered. (Darn insurance companies.) Instead, head for the **Oshkosh B'Gosh factory store** (Prime Outlets, 3001 S. Washburn, 920/426-5817), which features outlet prices.

ENTERTAINMENT AND EVENTS
The free monthly *The Scene* also lists Appleton and Green Bay happenings.

Bars and Music
Peabody's Ale House (544 N. Main St., 920/230-1110) has live music—blues to rock and jazz. For a basic watering hole without the cacophony of college students downing shots, try **Oblio's** (434 N. Main St., 920/426-1063). It's got a pressed-tin ceiling, an antique wood bar, and photos of old Oshkosh.

Cultural Events
Stage and theater shows are found on the campus of UW-Oshkosh at the **Frederic March Theatre** (926 Woodland Ave., 920/424-4417).

RECREATION
Fishing
Winnebago-region specialties are the white bass run (generally mid- to late May) and sheepshead. For a one-of-a-kind, only-in-Wisconsin experience, be here in February for the sturgeon spearing season.

Parks and Beaches
Asylum Point Park, a wildlife restoration area, has trails running from marshland to prairie to lakefront.

For swimming, jump in Lake Winnebago itself at **Menominee Park** along Millers Bay at Hazel and Merritt Streets. While there, sample the great zoo and "Little Oshkosh," one of the country's largest playgrounds and kiddie amusement parks.

Trail Systems
Of the 75 or so miles of multipurpose trail in the area, the main route is the **WIOUWASH Trail,** a crushed limestone surface meandering through woods, marshes, farm fields, and tallgrass prairie from Oshkosh to the Winnebago County line.

Camping
No state or county park camping options are very close. A private option is **Circle R Campground** (1185 Old Knapp Rd., 920/235-8909, $17); take exit WI 26 from U.S. 41 to Hwy. N and go east one mile.

ACCOMMODATIONS
Downtown
The least expensive option in downtown Oshkosh is the **Town Motel** (215 Division St., 920/233-0610, $50). Fresh coffee is the only extra.

STINKING WATER

Lake Winnebago dominates east-central Wisconsin. At 10 miles across and 30 miles north to south, this shallow lake – once a glacial marsh – is among the largest freshwater lakes fully locked within one state. It totals 88 miles of shoreline comprising 138,000 acres formed more than 25,000 years ago by a lobe of the Wisconsin glacier.

The lake was always crucial to Native Americans as a part of the water transport system along the Fox and Wolf Rivers. The name purportedly comes from a linguistic mix-up – or deliberate pejorative snub – from the French, who dubbed the Native American tribe they discovered here the "stinkers" (an updated transliteration); "Stinking Water" was a natural follow-up.

Lake Winnebago today is heavily populated with fishers and pleasure-crafters. In winter, up to 10,000 cars park on the frozen lake at any one time; if you're around in February, do not miss the annual throwback to Pleistocene days – the sturgeon-spearing season.

Wind east out of Fond du Lac via U.S. 151 to skirt the eastern shoreline along what locals call "the Ledge," the high breathtaking rise above Deadwood Point. The small town of Pipe along this route is home to an awesome 80-foot tower. Farther north is Calumet County Park, with six rare panther effigy mounds. (At the entrance to the park, stop at The Fish Tale Inn to see the largest male sturgeon ever caught on the lake.) An even better place to experience the lake is High Cliff State Park, along the northeastern edge.

There is another hotel lodging centrally located but it cannot be recommended for the price. What can be recommended, however, are the truly lovely rooms and welcoming proprietors of **Brayton B&B** (143 Church Ave., 920/267-0300, from $89).

West

Most Oshkosh accommodations are spread along the highway interchanges of U.S. 41 west of town. Cheapest of these is the always-economical **Marriott Fairfield Inn** (1800 S. Koeller Rd., 920/233-8504 or 800/228-2800, $70), off the 9th Street exit and offering a pool, whirlpool, and game room.

The **Hilton Garden Inn** (1355 W. 20th Ave., 920/966-1300, $84) is equidistant from attractions west and downtown and has a full slate of amenities.

FOOD

Supper Clubs and Fine Dining

The proprietors may dispute categorization as a supper club, but **Robbins** (1810 Omro Rd., 920/235-2840, 11 A.M.–10 P.M. Mon.–Sat., from 8 A.M. Sun., $7–19) closely fits the bill. Casual or formal, it's steaks and fresh fish; it also follows the Wisconsin tradition of in-house sausage-making and meat smoking.

Family Fare

Spacious but cozy, the **New Moon** (N. Main and Algoma Blvd., 920/232-0976, 7 A.M.–way late daily, $3–6), in a renovated 1875 beaut, is the place for coffee or a light meal. Sandwiches to creative soups (not your average offerings) are typical here—emphasizing local and state ingredients and products. It also offers live music and poetry readings.

Not far from Oshkosh, in little Omro, is the **Main Street Restaurant** (103 E. Main St., 920/685-5980, 5 A.M.–9 P.M. Mon.–Sat., 6 A.M.–8 P.M. Sun., $4 and up), housed in an 1881 grocery, shoe, and millinery store. Expect the occasional 40-pound turkeys and outstanding dressing to supplement the hearty family fare. You can also pick up a fishing lure at Al's Lure Shop, in a corner of the restaurant.

Drive-Ins

Oshkosh has two *classic* drive-ins. **Leon's** (121 W. Murdock Ave., 920/231-7755, 11 A.M.–11 P.M. Sun.–Thurs., till midnight Fri.–Sat. in summer) is a classic neon kind of place with delectable custards (and turtle sundaes!) and a mouthwatering homemade sloppy joe–style concoction. **Ardy and Ed's** (2413 S. Main St., 920/231-5455) has been around since 1948 and does not appear much changed. It still plays 1950s tunes, and the waitstaff still gets around aboard roller skates.

Fish Fries

Hands down, locals pick **Jeff's** (1005 Rugby St., 920/231-7450, dinner till 10 P.M. Mon.–Sat., lunch Fri. and Sun., breakfast Sun., $4–20) as the place to go for great seafood simultaneously down-home and cutting edge. The traditional perch at the Friday fish fry simply heads the list of seafood and steaks.

Brewpub

Fratello's Cafe is part of the complex of the **Fox River Brewing Company** (1501 Arboretum Dr., 920/232-2337, 11 A.M.–10 P.M. Mon.–Fri., 11 A.M.–11 P.M. Sat., 11 A.M.–9 P.M. Sun., $5). The attractive café interiors overlook the river; you can even boat up to the outdoor deck. Service has been iffy. Brewery tours are available Saturday.

Mexican

Head for **Lara's Tortilla Flats** (715 N. Main St., 920/233-4440, 11 A.M.–10 P.M. Mon.–Sat., $5–12), a real-deal family affair turning out excellent *norteño* food—the recipes came up with grandma from her Salinas boarding-house a century ago. (Everything's made from scratch.) The decor features images of the clan's role in the Mexican Revolution as well as great-grandpa's role in capturing legendary *bandito* Gregorio Cortez.

INFORMATION

The Oshkosh Convention and Visitors Bureau (920/303-9200 or 877/303-9200, www.visitoshkosh.com) is southwest of the U.S. 41 and WI 44 interchange along Waukau Avenue.

GETTING THERE

The local **Greyhound** stop is at Wittman Regional Airport (920/231-6490). Not too many buses serve Oshkosh.

Lamers bus line (800/261-6600) runs between Milwaukee and Wausau, with stops in Stevens Point, New London, Appleton, Oshkosh, and Fond du Lac.

Fond du Lac

Fond du Lac often refers to itself as "First on the Lake"—sort of a loose take on the French, which translates literally as "bottom (or far end) of the lake."

History

Three separate Winnebago villages predated European permanent arrival in 1785. Despite its strategic location—at the base of a big lake and equidistant to the Fox-Wisconsin riverway—the town grew painfully slowly. Everywhere-to-be-seen town father, and later Wisconsin's first territorial governor, James Doty, had the town platted in 1835.

Boomtown status effectively eluded the place—timber was too far north and receding fast. The local constabulary, the story goes, couldn't afford a pair of handcuffs! However, a plank road, laboriously laid down from Sheboygan, became a vital channel of transportation from the Lake Michigan coast.

FOND DU LAC

SIGHTS
Galloway House and Village

The stately mid-Victorian Italianate villa Galloway House (336 Old Pioneer Rd., 920/922-6390, 10 A.M.–4 P.M. daily Memorial Day weekend–Labor Day, $7 adults), originally finished in 1847, features 30 rooms, four fireplaces, and much Victorian opulence. Behind is a turn-of-the-20th-century village containing 23 restored regional dwellings and structures, including the Blakely Museum, an assortment of pioneer and early-20th-century Fond du Lac stuff, including an extensive local private Native American collection—even a mounted passenger pigeon.

EAST-CENTRAL WATERS

Octagon House

This 12-room private home (276 Linden St., 920/922-1608, www.octagonhousefdl.com, $15) was originally raised as a stockade against Native American attack. Later, it became a node on the Underground Railroad (you can add almost a dozen secret places to the number of rooms, including secret passages, tunnels, and one hidden room). And it wouldn't be complete without the requisite ghost reportedly wafting about. Tours must be arranged in advance.

St. Paul's Cathedral

This Episcopalian English Gothic stone cathedral (51 W. Division St., 920/921-3363, www.stpaulsepiscopalcathedral.org, 9 A.M.–4 P.M. Tues.–Fri., $2) houses the Oberammergau unified collection, a priceless assemblage of wood carvings. Tours are by appointment.

Lakeside Park

One of the better municipal parks anywhere is this 400-acre tract. The eastern part's eye-frying-white sentinel lighthouse is probably Fond du Lac's most recognizable symbol. Nearby are landscaped islands, a deer park, a minitrain, a harbor, and a marina, among other things. A carousel dating from the 1920s is one of the few extant wooden merry-go-rounds left in the state; it still runs on a simple two-gear clutch. All the horses are pegged—constructed wholly without nails.

Eldorado Marsh

Just a few miles west of Fond du Lac along WI 23 and Highway C is an unknown canoeists' paradise, the 6,000-acre Eldorado Marsh, which subsumes the 1,500-acre shallow flowage marsh. Locals refer to it as the "Everglades of the North." I'm not sure about that, but it is a tranquil, solitary spot.

EVENTS

Though it might get some argument from Port Washington to the southeast, Fond du Lac purports to hold the world's largest fish fry in June—more than 5,000 fish dinners and sandwiches are generally consumed in one gluttonous three-day **Walleye Weekend** (www.fdlfest.com).

RECREATION
Biking

The city has a balanced system of rural trails, including the great **Ledge Lookout Ride,** 45 miles on the eastern shore of Lake Winnebago along the Niagara Escarpment. Better yet is the **Wild Goose State Trail,** of which Fond du Lac is the northern terminus. The screened limestone trail stretches 34 miles south to the Horicon National Marsh, the city of Horicon, and beyond. A trail pass, which can be acquired at bike shops and some trailheads, is necessary.

Fishing

Fond du Lac is the southernmost access point for fishing on Lake Winnebago, the most popular fishing lake in the state. You gotta be here during sturgeon season!

ACCOMMODATIONS

Cheapest on the west side is the spartan **Stretch Eat and Sleep** (Pioneer Rd. at Hwy. OO and U.S. 41, 920/923-3131, $45–75), featuring air conditioning, a restaurant, and in-room computer access.

The **Microtel Inn and Suites** (649 W. Johnson St./WI 23, 920/929-4000 or 888/771-7171, $59) has a health club, whirlpool, and more.

The **Holiday Inn Holidome** (625 Rolling Meadows Dr., 920/923-1440 or 800/465-4329, $109) offers its usual amenities.

There's only one option near the central area, the full-service **Ramada Plaza Hotel** (1 N. Main St., 920/923-3000 or 800/272-6232, $119 s, $129 d). It has an indoor pool, whirlpool, lounge, restaurant, health club, covered parking, and some suites. And, according to a few visitors, some possibly paranormal activity!

FOOD
Burgers and Ice Cream

The teenybopping **Jukebox Charlie's** (248 N. Hickory St., 920/923-8185, open at 4 P.M.

Tues.–Sun., $5) features poodle-skirted waitresses, 1950s music on the jukebox, and a dance club, with occasional revue-type shows. There are burgers, malts, and the like, along with homemade tater chips! Outside, under a 35-foot jukebox sign, carhops move on wheels.

Since the Civil War, the family of **Kelley Country Creamery** (W5215 Hwy. B, 920/923-1715, daily) has been a dairy mainstay in these parts. You'll love their ice cream, especially sitting on a porch looking at the cows the milk came from! Head south on U.S. 41, then east on Highway B.

Supper Clubs and Fish Fries

If it's steak you want, head for **Sebastian's Steakhouse** (770 S. Main St., 920/922-3333, dinner daily, $4–14), which is certainly good for the number of choices it gives you and for the excellent value.

Jim and Linda's Lakeview (W3496 Hwy. W, 920/795-4116, www.jimandlindas.net, dinner daily in high season, dinner Tues.–Sun. off-season,$12–45) serves four-course dinners (and fish fries). If nothing else, come for the view of the lake—the place is 30 feet from the eastern shoreline. It's in little Pipe; take U.S. 151 east to Highway W and then west.

Italian

Bellafini's (7 14th St., 920/929-8909, dinner Tues.–Sat., $5–12) is a gem for Italian food and friendliness—so have said more than one Italian! That said, it can get a bit busy, so be patient.

Family Dining

Arguably *the* Lake Winnebago culinary institution is **◖ Schreiner's** (168 N. Pioneer Rd., 920/922-0590, 6:30 A.M.–8:30 P.M. daily, $3–9), a hearty American-style family restaurant serving meals since 1938. The menu is broad, the servings copious, and the specials Midwestern. But the real highlight is the bread, made fresh on-site in the bakery. The New England clam chowder is also superb—so good it's on the restaurant's website (www.fdlchowder.com).

INFORMATION

The Fond du Lac Area Convention and Visitors Bureau (171 S. Pioneer Rd., 920/923-3010 or 800/937-9123, www.fdl.com) is well stocked to help.

GETTING THERE

The local **Greyhound** stop (920/921-4215) is at the Mobil gas station, 976 South Main Street. **Lamers** (800/261-6600) also stops here on its run between Wausau and Milwaukee.

West of Winnebago

RIPON

One of the most picturesque small towns anywhere, winding Ripon has an oddball and fascinating heritage. Founded in 1844 by an organization called the Wisconsin Phalanx as an experiment in communal living, it was named Ceresco, after the Roman goddess of agriculture, and attempted to implement in pure form the democratic principles of French social progressive François Charles Marie Fourier. A decade later, it came to fame as the birthplace of the Republican Party. (This claim, incidentally, is hotly disputed by a few other communities in the United States, but hey, in 2004, the U.S.

Senate passed a bill recognizing Ripon's status, and even the U.S. Postal Service commemorated it with a postmark.)

Later, Ripon became the birthplace of another political pioneer—Carrie Chapman Catt, one of the founders and first presidents of both the American Women's Suffrage Association and the League of Women Voters; it was under her lead that the 19th Amendment to the Constitution was finally passed.

◖ The Little White Schoolhouse

Along the 300 block of Blackburn Street (WI 44) stands the birthplace of the Republican

the Little White Schoolhouse

© THOMAS HUHTI

Party, the Little White Schoolhouse (303 Blackburn St., 920/748-4730, 10 A.M.–4 P.M. daily June–Aug., weekends spring and fall, $1). This official national monument doesn't hold much more than a few mementos, but it's still fun to poke around in.

At the time of writing, rumor had it that adjacent to this a new **Republican Presidents Museum** was planned.

Other Sights
Ripon College (300 Seward St., 920/748-8364) overlooks the town from a hill and houses the C. J. Rodman Center for the Arts, containing two paintings by Sir Anthony Van Dyck.

Five miles or so south of town on WI 44/49, then east along Reed's Corner Road, is **Larson's Famous Clydesdales** (W12654 Reeds Corner Rd., 920/748-5466, Mon.–Sat. May–Oct., tours $15). More than a dozen of the equine giants made famous by sentimental Budweiser beer commercials are bred and raised here, including a national champion six-horse hitch. Demonstrations are given at 1 P.M., and visitors can pet the horses. Reservations are required.

GREEN LAKE
Green Lake is approximately one-sixth the size of Ripon, but this flyspeck town pulls in tons of visitors, all coming for the eponymous 7,320-acre lake—the deepest in the state, if not the largest. In 1867, the first resort west of Niagara Falls was built here. When Chicagoans heard about it, the rush was on. Within three decades, posh resorts had begun to dot the shores. Despite its granddaddy status as a resort, the tourists are neither condescending bluebloods nor so numerous that the small-town charm is obliterated.

Sights
Explore local history in Friday Park (along Mill St.) at an old **railroad depot** housing historic artifacts; architecturally even more appealing are the historic 1910 **Thrasher Opera House** (506 Mill St.) and 1898 **Green Lake County Courthouse** (492 Hill St.).

On the water, Heidel House Resort operates the popular **Escapade Tours** (643 Illinois Ave., 920/294-3344, $13). Brunch, cocktail, dinner, and sightseeing excursions are also offered.

Scenic Drive

Rustic Road 22, also known as White River Road, ends at Highway D, north of Princeton, but affords the experience of two original plank bridges and views of mostly DNR-protected wetlands. From Green Lake, head west along WI 23 to Princeton, then north on Highway D.

Speaking of Princeton, do check out this little treasure. It's a time-locked little burg plunked along the Fox River and has plenty of anachronistic architecture, worthy galleries, and the state's largest weekly flea market. Princeton is also site of the long-running **Cattle Fair.** For ice cream and light foods, you can check out, let's see, a refurbished gas station or renovated general store; or find excellent Italian food (along with tarot cards) in a 19th-century Victorian at **Mimi's** (523 Water St., 920/295-6775, lunch and dinner daily, $6–15).

Or how about a drive with an eco-bent? A number of miles west of the little town of Montello, then south on Highway F, takes you to **Muir Park and Fountain Lake Farm,** the boyhood home of John Muir as well as a birder's paradise. Many sandhill cranes can be seen here—the Fox River Unit of the Horicon National Wildlife Refuge is across the road. It's estimated that Marquette County alone holds one of North America's highest concentrations, about 1,100.

Recreation

There's an awful lot to do in Green Lake, but fishing tops the list (though the golf ain't bad either). The **Green Lake Marina** (485 Park Dr., 920/294-6221) rents all craft.

For land-based recreation, there may be more golf courses per capita in the Green Lake vicinity than anywhere in Wisconsin. The Scottish links style **Golf Courses of Lawsonia** (WI 23 W, 920/294-3320) have been rated as among America's top public courses, according to *Golf Digest* magazine, which gave the elevated tees and merciless bunkers four stars. The **Tuscumbia Country Club** (680 N. Illinois

EAST-CENTRAL WATERS

BIRTH OF THE REPUBLICAN PARTY

By the early 1850s, regarding slavery the powers within the contemporary political parties were impotent, willfully ignorant or hamstrung by both sides. Antislavery activists within the Whig Party in Ripon ultimately grew tired enough to call for action. In 1852, Alvan Earle Bovay visited Horace Greeley in New York City to discuss matters. The Whigs were waning, but what was next?

Then, Senator Stephen Douglass of Illinois provided an opportunity for a minor revolution with his Kansas-Nebraska Bill; the proposal was to extend slavery beyond the perimeters of the earlier Missouri Compromise.

Bovay immediately and quietly summoned 53 other voters back to Ripon to devise a battle plan for opposing the slavery proponents. Ripon had long been a nerve center of the abolitionist movement. So strong was its opposition, in fact, that the city was the site of what's known as "Booth's War," a guerrilla skirmish between Milwaukee abolitionist Sherman Booth, who helped escaped slaves along the Underground Railroad, and the federal authorities; local citizens helped Booth and frustrated the authorities for a five-year period.

Bovay hoped to organize the abolitionists into a cohesive force to be called Republicans ("a good name...with charm and prestige," he said). His oratory was effective, and the Republican Party was born on March 20, 1854, in the Little White Schoolhouse in Ripon. Official declaration of its platform came two years later in Pittsburgh; standing near the podium was Abraham Lincoln, who, four years later, would become the party's first successful presidential candidate.

Ave., 920/294-3240) is Wisconsin's oldest course; it's known as one of the best-manicured courses in the Midwest.

Accommodations

Rates are *really* high around here during the summer.

A motel with a resort complex sums up **Bay View** (439 Lake St., 920/294-6504, $105), a good deal for the money. Anglers love this place—there's plenty of fishing and boat rentals. Some kitchenettes and suites are available.

One of Wisconsin's best and best-known resorts is the (**Heidel House Resort** (643 Illinois Ave., 920/294-6128 or 800/444-2812, www.heidel house.com, $165–615), a 20-acre, self-contained sybaritic universe. More than 200 guest rooms, including some estate buildings, run the gamut of luxury—it even plunked down $200 million for a new spa. The dining is superb.

Both **Miller's Daughter** (453 North St., 920/294-0717, www.millersdaughter.com, $155) and **Angel Inn** (372 S. Lawson Dr., 920/294-3087, www.angelinns.com, from $115) are superb bed and breakfasts—truly special, each of them, so take your pick.

Food

A local favorite is **Norton's** (380 S. Lawson Dr., 920/294-6577, lunch and dinner daily, $9–28), the only supper club on the lake accessible by water. Norton's has grand alfresco dining on a lakeside deck.

Ready to splurge? Rated one of the best restaurants in Wisconsin is the (**Grey Rock Mansion Restaurant** (643 Illinois Ave., 920/294-6128 or 800/444-2812, www.heidel-house.com, dinner Tues.–Sat., brunch Sun., dinner Thurs.–Sat. in off-season) in the Heidel House Resort and Conference Center. Housed in an 1890s building, the charming rich woods interiors and fireplaces support the food. The walleye here will knock your socks off.

Information

The **Green Lake Area Chamber of Commerce** (550 Mill St., 920/294-3231 or 800/253-7354, www.visitgreenlake.com) is in town.

WAUPACA AND THE CHAIN O' LAKES

The Waupaca area lies at the western edge of the east-central waters region and qualifies as hydrophilic: 22 spring-fed lakes southwest of Waupaca form one of the longest recreational stretches in the lower half of Wisconsin—240 lakes in the county alone. Settlement began in the region around 1848; the first flour mill went up a year after the state's birth. The city was named for an altruistic Potawatomi chief, Sam Waupaca, who collapsed and died after convincing local Natives not to kill the white settlers.

Sights

The most popular activity in the Chain O' Lakes is to take a breezy ride aboard an authentic sternwheeler, the former flagship of a brewery, the *Chief* (or on the more sedate motor yacht *Lady of the Lakes*). The 90-minute tours take in 8–11 lakes of the chain. Sunday champagne brunch tours ($14) are available. **Tours** (715/258-2866) begin running Memorial Day weekend and depart four times daily 11:30 A.M.–4 P.M. for the eight-lake tour aboard the *Chief*; rates run $10 adults. There are fewer departures during the weeks before Memorial Day and after Labor Day. The 11-lake tour on the *Lady of the Lakes* costs the same and lasts two hours; it departs at 4 P.M.

Just southwest of Waupaca along WI 22 lies tiny **Rural,** honest to goodness a town that time forgot. It's a Yankee town stuck in the middle 1800s. Virtually the entire city, along the switchbacking banks of the Crystal River, is on the National Register of Historic Places. The architectural renaissance is impressive; it's gotten so popular that WI 22 was rerouted around the town to avoid spoiling it. It's also a good spot to pick up antiques. Check out the unbelievable selection at **Walker's Barn,** a converted chicken farm that now seems to have about half the antiques in Waupaca County.

Another short jaunt out of the city via Highway K takes you to **Red Mill.** The biggest waterwheel in the state, it's been converted into a hodgepodge of shops offering handicrafts, antiques, and lots and lots of scented candles in an original interior. One of the few extant covered bridges in Wisconsin is also there (400 handcrafted oak pegs were used in its construction), along with the Chapel in the Woods. Red Mill lies along a beautiful stretch of the Crystal River with a picturesque park.

Scenic Drives

Two of those farm-to-market narrow country lanes in the area are **Rural Road** and **Emmons Creek Road,** both jutting westward out of Rural toward Hartman Creek State Park. The former serpentines across the Crystal River several times; the latter takes in a tributary trout stream of the Crystal and lots of woodland.

South of Waupaca along Highway E (itself fairly narrow) is Saxeville and, still farther south, **26th Road,** along Highway W out of town; 26th Road stretches to Highway H along the Pine River Valley, a Class II trout stream. This drive passes several dwellings—one a log cabin—predating the Civil War.

Recreation

A segment of the National Scenic Ice Age Trail is in **Hartman Creek State Park** (715/258-2372); the county section totals 20 miles and links on both ends with Portage County's segment. The park has a hike-in primitive cabin offered on a first-come, first-served basis. The state park also maintains off-road bike trails. The park is also popular with canoeists and boaters, since most of the upper Chain O' Lakes are either in or adjacent to state park lands.

The lolling, tranquil Crystal River is perfect for canoeing. Organized excursions leave from **Ding's Dock** (along Hwy. Q, 715/258-2612), which also rents decent cottages.

This is prime touring area for bikers; trails run along waterways and through some Amish farmstead areas. Northwest of the city, the topography shifts to rolls of kettles and moraines.

Camping

Hartman Creek State Park is the best bet for camping. Otherwise, in or near the city are six private campgrounds, including some in town: **Waupaca Camping Park** (E2411 Holmes Rd., 715/258-8010, $20) has separate tent areas.

Accommodations

This is another resort/cottage area, so despite the large numbers of places, few are cheap. More upscale lodging is at the **Best Western Grand Seasons** (110 Grand Seasons Dr., junction of WI 10 and 54, 715/258-9212 or 887/880-1054, $79), which has a pool, health club, sauna, and enormous game room.

In anachronistic Rural (*the* place for a quaint getaway) is the ◖ **Crystal River Inn** (E1369 Rural Rd., 715/258-5333 or 800/236-5789, www.crystal-riverinn.com, $70–168), an old farmstead. The six original farmhouse guest rooms (with myriad styles and amenities) are done with antiques and brass beds. All the rooms have views of either the river, a wildwood garden, or the backyard garden. You'll also find cottages and a "Little House on the Prairie." Superb.

Food and Entertainment

The Clear Water Harbor (N2757 Hwy. QQ, 715/258-2866, www.clearwaterharbor.com, from 10 A.M. daily, $3), known locally as the "Har Bar," serves a menu varying from pub grub sandwiches (try its famous 'shroomburger') to salads and a Friday fish fry. It's also popular for summer entertainment, with a huge deck on the lakeside. It's open seasonally. From here, you can do the Wally Walk up the road into King to the very local **Wally's Bar** (N2702 County Rd. QQ, 715/258-2160), where you can get a Lunch Box shot: beer with amaretto and orange juice. (It's tasty if you can down it quickly.)

A respectable eatery (a place you'd take your grandma) is **Simpson's** (222 S. Main St., 715/258-2330, lunch and dinner daily, $4 and up), a subdued supper club also known as the Indian Room. Simpson's has been serving lunch and dinner since the 1930s, specializing in chicken with mushrooms and wine sauce.

Information

The **Waupaca Area Chamber of Commerce** (221 S. Main St., 715/258-7343 or 888/417-4040, www.waupacamemories.com) has all the info you need.

The Wolf River Region

MENOMINEE INDIAN RESERVATION

The Menominee nation represents the oldest established inhabitants of the territory of Wisconsin. Unlike the diasporic nature of many U.S. tribes, the Menominee are strictly Wisconsin residents. The reservation lies a chipshot north of Shawano and abuts the southern perimeter of the Chequamegon-Nicolet National Forest and the northern edge of the much smaller Stockbridge Indian Reservation. All Wisconsinites nod at its crown jewel, the Wolf River, one of the region's top draws.

History

Anthropologists have surmised that the Menominee, an Algonquian-speaking tribe, may have been in the Wisconsin territory as far back as 10,000 years ago. The tribe and its many bands once controlled regions of the Upper Great Lakes from as far south as Milwaukee to the Escanaba River in Michigan's Upper Peninsula and the entire breadth of Wisconsin.

Beginning in 1817, a series of breached federal treaties gradually eroded Menominee sovereignty until, by 1854, they were allowed only 12 townships on the present-day reservation; some of the ceded land was turned over to the Oneida and Stockbridge Indians for their own reservations. Almost 10 million acres dwindled to 200,000.

The Menominee, who had been given reservation status by a treaty signed near the Wolf River's Keshena Falls, asked for their status as natives to be terminated in 1961 in an attempt at federal assimilation. It was a dismal failure, and reservation status was reinstated in 1973. The tribe today numbers approximately 6,500, more than half of whom live on the reservation.

Menominee Indian Reservation Forest

The 223,500 acres of forest surrounding the reservation include some of the most pristine stands of hardwoods, hemlock, and pine in the Great Lakes region; it's regarded as an invaluable ecosystem. The tribe has had a lumber operation since 1908, one of the first and largest Native-owned in the United States; they had been trading lumber with the Winnebago long before European contact. Their high-tech present-day plant is the largest and most modern in the region. More than two billion board feet have been removed from the forest—more than twice the entire yield. Yet the Menominee have been lauded by international environmentalists for instituting a radical sustainable ecosystem model, now being examined by Indian bands from the Atlantic Coast to the Nuu-chah-nulth group of tribes from Vancouver Island. Forestry experts from as far away as Cambodia and Indonesia have come to the tribe's new forestry institute.

◖ Wolf River

Meandering through the reservation from its headwaters in Lily to the north is the nascent Wolf River, a part of the Fox River system, which includes the Fox and Wolf Rivers headwaters, the lower Fox River, and Lake Winnebago. Quiet at its source, it picks up steam as it crosses through Langlade, and by the time it hits the reservation, it's got a bit of a dander up. This stretch of the state-designated Outstanding Water Resource and federally-designated wild river is perhaps the most spectacular. It drops almost 1,000 feet as it crosses the reservation, from the multihued juttings and white water of Smokey Falls to the eerie canyons of the Wolf River Dells. Water conditions range from placid—below Post Lake—to hair-raising—in sections near Smokey Falls.

The colorful toponymy describes it well: Little Slough Gundy, Sherry Rapids, Horse Race Rapids, Twenty Day Rips, and more. The stretch of river between Gilmore's Mistake and Smokey Falls—the lower terminus for most rafters—can be rife with midrange rapids, some up to eight feet.

So pristine are these waters that the Wolf River was the inspiration for the state's most enduring environmental debate—whether or not a mine to the northwest in Crandon would endanger the ecology. And in terms of recreation—these waters are, indeed, blue ribbon for rafters and kayakers.

The river has sections for neophytes and for hard-core river runners. (During high-water periods, operators shut down trips—proof it can be serious business.) Outfitters in these parts generally don't supply guides or captains, so you're on your own. White-water enthusiasts also note: The Red River nearby—Gresham, especially—is also quite good for kayaking.

There are a handful of tour operators in the area; many just rent boats, while others run full six-hour trips. Most offer camping. **River Forest Rafts** (715/882-3351, www.wolfriver-camping.com) has watercraft/bike rentals and has trails for mountain bikes.

Operating out of Keshena on the Menominee Indian Reservation is **Big Smokey Falls Rafting** (715/799-3359), with three runs between the W. W. Bridge paralleling WI 55 through three falls areas.

For a one-of-a-kind lodging option, try ◖ **Jesse's Historic Wolf River Lodge** (W2119 Taylor Rd., 715/882-2182, www.wolfriverlodge.com, $100–300) in White Lake. Rustic deep woods relaxing best describes it. There are lodge rooms, various cabins, even a funky tree house that is beyond description. All rooms come with a rib-sticking breakfast.

Off the river and aside roads, the Wolf River is worth investigating on foot. **Wolf River Dells** has a short nature trail leading to rough multicolored granite cliffs overlooking the Wolf for hundreds of yards along both the upper and lower dells. The Dells are four miles from a well-marked turnoff from WI 55 along a road that alternates from hardpack gravel to nerve-wracking. A footbridge crosses the 40-foot gurgling Smokey Falls to a small midriver island. Purportedly, the mist from the waters is actually smoke from the pipe of a spirit living within the falls. **Spirit Rock,** a couple of miles above Keshena Falls, is also significant.

According to legend it's really a petrified Menominee warrior who angered the earth. This warrior, Ko-Ko-Mas-Say-Sa-Now, allegedly asked for immortality and was thrust into the earth forever. Some believe kind spirits come to offer rings of tobacco, and their willowy vapors can be observed flitting among the trees in the dusky night.

Oh, don't forget fishing. One of Wisconsin's designated fly-fishing-only stretches of blue-ribbon trout waters is near Hollister.

Menominee Logging Camp Museum

The Menominee Logging Camp Museum (Hwy VV, north of Keshena, 715/799-3757, 9 A.M.–3 P.M. Tues.–Sat., 11 A.M.–4 P.M. Sun., May 1–Oct. 15, $10 adults), at Grignon Rapids along the Wolf River, north of the Wolf at Highway VV along WI 47, is the largest and most comprehensive exhibit of timber heritage in the United States (it is also pricey). Seven hand-hewn log buildings and more than 20,000 artifacts re-create an early 1900s logging camp. The rustic feel adds to the experience. Of note are the 12-to-a-bunk bunkhouse and the 1,000 pairs of oxen shoes, not to mention a 400-year-old pine log.

Powwows

Two powwows are held annually. On (or close to) Memorial Day weekend, the **Veteran Powwow** honors the reservation's military veterans. Larger is the **Annual Menominee Nation Contest Powwow,** held the first weekend in August. This is one of the largest cultural events in the Upper Midwest. Both are held in the natural amphitheater Woodland Bowl.

STOCKBRIDGE-MUNSEE INDIAN RESERVATION

The Stockbridge-Munsee are an Algonquian-speaking band of the Mohican Indians. The three tribes composing the band (along with a fourth, which eventually opted for assimilation) stretch throughout the Connecticut and Hudson River Valleys. This band is one of the best traveled of any in the state, though that's hardly of its own doing; the word "Mohican" means, aptly enough, "people of never-still waters." They first appeared in Wisconsin in the early 1820s, living in the Fox River Valley (hence, the town of Stockbridge on the eastern shore of Lake Winnebago; the Stockbridge cemetery there is a National Historic Site) along with the Munsee, a Delaware tribe also forced west by European expansion. Some Stockbridge Indians decamped to Indiana Territory in Kansas; others moved to Red Springs, Wisconsin, to live on land ceded to them in 1856 by the Menominee (who got $20,000 for 2.5 million acres). The tribe numbers about 1,500.

Sights

The **Stockbridge Munsee Historical Library Museum** (715/793-4270, 8 A.M.–4:30 P.M. Mon.–Fri., free) has one of the best archives of Native American material in Wisconsin, including maps dating from the 1600s (not on public display). Most exhibits are on the day-to-day life of the Stockbridge and the later fur trade. Of note is the section on the missionaries—those stoic Jesuits—including a catechism written in Mohican and a 1745 Bible presented to the Stockbridge by an emissary of the Prince of Wales. The library and museum are four miles east of Bowler.

SHAWANO

Shawano lies along the proud Wolf River at one of its widest points and serves as the recreational heart of the Wolf. The lake bearing the name Shawano sits to the east, full of fish.

The name (pronounced SHAW-no) is another mellifluous result of the Menominee term for the large lake: Sha-Wah-Nah-Pay-Sa, "Lake to the South."

Settlers first came to work in lumber mills built in the 1840s and then to serve traffic on an old military road (Main Street was part of it). The city now has one of the country's largest milk-products plants and a leading artificial breeding cooperative.

But it's recreation that draws most

visitors—fishing on Shawano Lake and whitewater rafting on the wild Wolf River. This is true-blue, mom-and-pop, basic family-style resort country.

Sights

The **Heritage Park Museum** (524 N. Franklin St., 715/526-3536, 1:30–4:30 P.M. Sat.–Sun. in summer, $3 adults) adjoins the Wolf River and Sunset Island downtown on a somewhat dusty compound. The museum features cheesemaking exhibits and a collection of early street lamps, among other buildings. The downtown also has a restored old depot with assorted historical flotsam.

Seven miles south of town, the almost unknown **Navarino Wildlife Area** is a restored 1,400-acre glacial lakebed, once a swamp and wetland that was drained and farmed for a century. Fifteen dikes have re-created the wetlands—sedge meadow to cattail marsh. Prairie and oak savanna restoration work is ongoing. The marshes support a resident family of sandhill cranes; the best wildlife-viewing is along the Wolf River drainages on the western fringes, near McDonald Road. A nature center (715/526-4226, Mon. and Fri. only) is at the site. Get to the wildlife area via WI 156 and McDonald Road.

The **Mielke Theater** (715/526-6171) stands in an isolated, bucolic setting with a country garden and offers year-round cultural events varying from an arts and crafts fair (a good time to scout for Midwestern handicrafts) to children's theater and plenty of concerts. Go a mile north on WI 29 and then follow signs along Highway HHH.

Scenic Drives

Definitely pick up a great map of the *Pineries to the Present* state heritage tours (four!). The tours are fully detailed and worth a whole day of checking out extant sights in two counties!

West of Shawano approximately 25 miles is tiny **Wittenburg,** the endpoint of one of Wisconsin's Rustic Roads, this one Highway M, which ends in **Tigerton.** There are lovely scenes on this route—historic round barns and stone buildings (including a gas station), and closet-size historical museums in both Wittenburg and Tigerton.

Tigerton was also the home of Wisconsin's first antigovernment militia, the Posse Comitatus, who made some waves in the early 1980s before retreating into obscurity after several of its leaders were jailed. They've been pretty quiet since, though there are definitely still members out there. An important thing to remember in these days of militias under every rock is that these folks have always been around.

Events

Every August, Shawano hosts three days of fiddlin' and pickin' during the **Folk Festival** (www.shawanoarts.com) at Mielke Theater and Park. Featured in prior years have been national folk acts, along with such diverse activities as Japanese *koto* and tea ceremonies.

Recreation

The **Mountain Bay Trail** is a 65-mile multi-use trail connecting Green Bay, Shawano, and Wausau. It's a grand trail and leads to numerous other trails. Ditto with the **WIOUWASH Trail**, which intersects with the Mountain Bay Trail in Eland.

Closest public **camping** is on the north shore of Shawano Lake, via Highway H, with 90 campsites in a decent wooded area with a great big beach. Sites run $11.

Accommodations

A good budget option is the strictly motel **Pine Acre** (1346 E. Green Bay St., 715/524-6665 or 800/730-5236, $45), with few amenities but excellently appointed rooms (and one cottage) and low prices. It's on a nicely wooded lot.

Most of Shawano is classic Wisconsin rustic lodging country—cabins and cottages that are clean but very, very simple. Rates vary: You can find a cabin for four folks for as low as $600 a week—not a bad deal. A good example of Shawano lodging is **Bamboo Shores** (W5873 Cedar Ave., 715/524-2124 or 800/969-2124, $1,000–2,000 per week), which has cottages that can sleep 6–10.

Food

A popular supper club with a few creative twists on the menu (duck confit, for example) is **Cotton Patch** (W4890 Lake Dr., 715/745-2101, dinner Wed.–Sun., brunch Sun., $8–22); they also have live entertainment Friday and Saturday.

It's strictly German food at **Sigrid's Bavarian Trail** (Hwy. H on Loon Lake Dr., 715/745-2660, lunch and dinner Tues.–Sun., $6–12), which also has live entertainment and a German deli, all overlooking Loon Lake.

Information

The visitors center of the chamber of commerce (213 E. Green Bay St., 715/524-2139 or 800/235-8528, www.shawanocountry.com) is well-stocked for you!

www.moon.com

DESTINATIONS | ACTIVITIES | BLOGS | MAPS | BOOKS

MOON.COM is ready to help plan your next trip! Filled with fresh trip ideas and strategies, author interviews, informative travel blogs, a detailed map library, and descriptions of all the Moon guidebooks, Moon.com is all you need to get out and explore the world—or even places in your own backyard. While at Moon.com, sign up for our monthly e-newsletter for updates on new releases, travel tips, and expert advice from our on-the-go Moon authors. As always, when you travel with Moon, expect an experience that is uncommon and truly unique.

MOON IS ON FACEBOOK—BECOME A FAN!
JOIN THE MOON PHOTO GROUP ON FLICKR

MAP SYMBOLS

▨▨▨	Expressway	🄲	Highlight	✈	Airfield	⚲	Golf Course
▬▬▬	Primary Road	○	City/Town	✈	Airport	🅿	Parking Area
▬▬	Secondary Road	◉	State Capital	▲	Mountain	▰	Archaeological Site
▭▭▭	Unpaved Road	⊛	National Capital	✦	Unique Natural Feature	▮	Church
------	Trail	★	Point of Interest			🚰	Gas Station
⋯⋯⋯	Ferry	•	Accommodation	🐋	Waterfall	⬯	Glacier
▬·▬·▬	Railroad	▼	Restaurant/Bar	⚑	Park	◺	Mangrove
▩▩▩	Pedestrian Walkway	▪	Other Location	🄣	Trailhead	▨	Reef
⸽⸽⸽⸽⸽	Stairs	Λ	Campground	🎿	Skiing Area	⬚	Swamp

CONVERSION TABLES

°C = (°F - 32) / 1.8
°F = (°C x 1.8) + 32
1 inch = 2.54 centimeters (cm)
1 foot = 0.304 meters (m)
1 yard = 0.914 meters
1 mile = 1.6093 kilometers (km)
1 km = 0.6214 miles
1 fathom = 1.8288 m
1 chain = 20.1168 m
1 furlong = 201.168 m
1 acre = 0.4047 hectares
1 sq km = 100 hectares
1 sq mile = 2.59 square km
1 ounce = 28.35 grams
1 pound = 0.4536 kilograms
1 short ton = 0.90718 metric ton
1 short ton = 2,000 pounds
1 long ton = 1.016 metric tons
1 long ton = 2,240 pounds
1 metric ton = 1,000 kilograms
1 quart = 0.94635 liters
1 US gallon = 3.7854 liters
1 Imperial gallon = 4.5459 liters
1 nautical mile = 1.852 km

ABOUT THE AUTHOR

Thomas Huhti

Thomas Huhti is a native Cheesehead who wound up studying in China during university – itchy feet and wanderlust have been a familial curse – which ultimately led to a five-year stint traveling the globe and living out of a backpack. A fortuitous meeting with a travel scribe on a Chinese mountain opened the then-young punk's eyes quite wide to the possibilities of combining travel and writing – his two loves – as a career.

But half a decade wandering the world made him long for his birthplace, about which, sadly, he realized he knew precious little. A four-year pilgrimage around the state to research the first edition of *Moon Wisconsin* became a gift to his parents, worthy Badgers both. Ultimately, he discovered he bled Badger red and understood where "home" really was.

Now it's a lifelong labor of love (at least outside of deadline crunch times). With his navigator-partner, Yuki, and his bigheaded yellow lab, Bobo, fighting over who gets to ride shotgun, the tent drying in the back of the car, and a Brewers game on the radio, Thomas can be found wandering Wisconsin's highways, searching for yet another lake.

MOON SPOTLIGHT WISCONSIN'S DOOR COUNTY

Avalon Travel
a member of the Perseus Books Group
1700 Fourth Street
Berkeley, CA 94710, USA
www.moon.com

Editor and Series Manager: Kathryn Ettinger
Copy Editor: Naomi Adler Dancis
Graphics Coordinator: Kathryn Osgood
Production Coordinators: Sean Bellows and
 Domini Dragoone
Cover Designer: Domini Dragoone
Map Editor: Brice Ticen
Cartographer: Kat Bennett

ISBN: 978-1-59880-765-3

Text © 2011 by Thomas Huhti.
Maps © 2011 by Avalon Travel.
All rights reserved.

Front cover photo: Rock Island State Park
 © DoorCounty.com/Door County Visitor Bureau
Title page image: Highway 42 near Northport
 in Door County, © Door County Chamber of
 Commerce

Printed in Canada by Friesens